WRITING FROM THE BODY

Facing the Fire
At My Father's Wedding
The Flying Boy
Flying Boy Book II
A Quiet Strength

WRITING
FROM THE
BODY

For Writers, Artists, and
Dreamers
Who Long to Free Your Voice

JOHN LEE
with Ceci Miller-Kritsberg

St. Martin's Press
New York

Grateful acknowledgement is made for permission to reprint selections from the following:

"Danse Russe" by William Carlos Williams: *The Collected Poems of William Carlos Williams, 1939–1962*, vol. II. Copyright © 1962 by William Carlos Williams. Reprinted by permission of New Directions Publishing Corp.

Reprint from *First You have to Row a Little Boat: Reflections on Life and Living* by Richard Bode. Copyright © 1992 by Richard Bode. Reprinted by permission of Warner Books, Inc.

Reprint from *Fried Green Tomatoes at the Whistle Stop Cafe* by Fannie Flagg. Copyright © 1987 by Fannie Flagg. Reprinted by permission of Random House, Inc.

Reprint from "From March '79" © 1987 by Robert Hass. From *Thomas Transtromer, Selected Poems 1954–1986*, ed. by Robert Hass. Reprinted by permission of The Ecco Press.

"If I Could Be Like Wallace Stevens" by William Stafford, from *The Darkness Around Us Is Deep* by William Stafford. Copyright © 1993 by William Stafford. Reprinted by permission of HarperCollins Publishers, Inc.

"In a Dark Time" by Theodore Roethke, from *The Collected Poems of Theodore Roethke* by Theodore Roethke. Copyright © 1960 by Beatrice Roethke, Administratrix of the Estate of Theodore Roethke. Reprinted by permission of Doubleday, a division of Bantam Doubleday Dell Puslishing Group, Inc.

Reprint from quatrain #116 of *Open Secret* by Rumi, translated from the Persian by John Moyne and Coleman Barks. Copyright © 1984 by John Moyne and Coleman Barks. Reprinted by permission of Threshold Books, RD 4 Box 600, Putney, VT.

Reprint from *Owning Your Own Shadow* by Robert Johnson. Copyright © 1991 by Robert Johnson. Reprinted by permission of HarperCollins Publishers, Inc.

"The Still Time" by Galway Kinnell, from *Mortal Acts, Mortal Words* by Galway Kinnell. Copyright © 1980 by Galway Kinnell. Reprinted by permission of Houghton Mifflin Co.

Reprint from *Ulysses* by James Joyce. Copyright © 1986 by Random House, Inc.

"Warning to the Reader" by Robert Bly, from *What Have I Ever Lost by Dying* by Robert Bly. Copyright © 1992 by Robert Bly. Reprinted by permission of HarperCollins Publishers, Inc.

Design by Richard Oriolo

LIBRARY OF CONGRESS CATALOGING-IN-PUBLICATION DATA

Lee, John H.
    Writing from the body / John Lee with Ceci Miller-Kritsberg.
    p. cm.
    ISBN 0-312-11536-9
    1. Authorship. 2. Meditations. I. Miller-Kritsberg, Ceci.
    II. Title.
    PN145.L34 1994
    808'.02—dc20   94–34702
                                                               CIP

10 9 8 7 6 5 4 3 2

Dedicated to Bill Stott

*Dismiss what insults your own soul, and your
very flesh shall be a great poem.*

—WALT WHITMAN

CONTENTS

Contents

ACKNOWLEDGMENTS

I would not have written this book or any other if it hadn't been for Bill Stott, Betty Sue Flowers, Robert Bly, Mrs. Timmons, my mother—Frances Lee and another dozen or two poets, playwrights, novelists, psychologists, and psychotherapists.

I thank those who have written some of the best books on writing and thus inspired and influenced me: Natalie Goldberg, Brenda Ueland, and Susan Shaughnessy.

I want to express my deep appreciation to Jared Kieling for believing in me and this project enough to get me to St. Martin's Press and to my editor, George Witte, and his assistant, Ann McKay Farrell, for their time, patience, and talents.

Most of all I want to thank two people whom I love dearly: Wayne Kritsberg for the support he gave me and Ceci on this project not to mention his invaluable advice, and Ceci Miller Kritsberg for being not only easy and a delight to work with but for the deep friendship and creativity she gave willingly and wonderfully.

I deeply appreciate my partner, Bev Barnes, for supporting my writing and for believing in me.

—John Lee

Acknowledgments

Heartfelt thanks to all the authors whose work appears in excerpt form in this book.

Thanks to John for being so much fun to work with, and to Jared Kieling for gently guiding the direction of the book. To Tracy Daugherty, for hints and teachings, and for suggesting wonderful fiction excerpts. Thanks to Tim Seibles (and Corona Press) for the poem "The Body Knew," for clarifying our debt to the physical self, and its sanctity.

With deep gratitude, I mention the writing teachers whose instruction awakened me to write from the body: Michael Ryan, Jack Myers, John Skoyles, Cynthia Macdonald, Donald Justice, and *especially* Marvin Bell.

To Wayne and Matthew Kritsberg, for their patient support and understanding.

Loving thanks to my mother for reading poems to me, and for her conviction in the power of language as art.

I thank the sweet grace that fuels my life and grants every word.

—Ceci Miller-Kritsberg

PREFACE

This book is about helping you to discover your own body of writing, to help you begin to experience your physical self as an endless creative well from which to draw amazing drink, regardless of your age, writing experience, or educational background. Whether you are a student of literature, a dramatist working on a tough bit of dialogue, or a parent who wants to turn a bedtime story into a children's book, the techniques introduced here will be of service to you. This book has something for the writer of advertising copy, the journalist, the songwriter, and that nearly extinct artist: the letter writer.

For veteran writers seeking to break through the body armoring that has prevented their work from realizing its greatest possibilities, this book offers exercises as well as explanations. For would-be writers challenging long-held beliefs that only "born artists" can write, this book can be a doorway to your Creative Self. For both kinds of writers—the fledgling and the bird in the air—this book offers encouragement to enter your body's mysteries for the sake of finding your personal truth.

This book is not going to teach you how to write in the same way that most writing manuals promise to do. Rather, this book will help clarify why we don't write or create in general, and will aid your discovery of the blocks in your body that are keeping your voice locked away, unable to be heard by you or by anyone else. We'll uncover the messages of people we revered, trusted, or rivaled, who gave us to understand that we didn't *know* how to create. We'll erase those messages and replace them with the truth: we all have at least one book hiding in the body. This is a book to read before you plunge into the "how to write" books, many of which are listed at the back of this one.

In this book you'll learn the grammar of the gut, the syntax of the sinews, the language of the legs. You'll see that structure comes from the skeleton and content from caring about your core truths. You'll learn ways to communicate from your chest, from your back, from your pelvis, and, ultimately, from all of these—from your deepest Self.

You won't necessarily learn how to publish anything. You certainly won't be taught to become a critic. But you will learn how to produce prose and poetry that will keep you creatively alive. You may get your work published in the process; but even if you do not, you'll understand how to listen to yourself before you listen to constructive criticism from others. You'll discover how not to take that criticism into your body.

This book is for everyone who is creating and writing now, and for everyone who wants to write but hasn't been able to find the truest words. It is especially for those whose fears have stopped them. Here are what I call "The Eight Great Fears":

1. *Fear of Being Left Alone*

2. *Fear of Offending*

3. *Fear of Showing All of Ourselves*

4. *Fear of Our Own Shadow*

5. *Fear of the Mud and the Blood*

6. *Fear of Success*

7. Fear of Failure/of Not Getting Published

8. Fear of Trust

This book seeks to explain these fears, and to illuminate how they block our best impulses, our best writing. These fears have become "great" because we've given them the power to dictate our choices for us. Here, in this list, they stand unchallenged, the same way they sit on our hearts. We're going to change that. Now that we have them up on a pedestal where we can see them, it's time to explain to each of them that they're going to have to get off and get out. Thanks for the memories.

For everyone who is tired of living life in the little closet between the ears, get ready. Together we'll do an overdue housecleaning. We'll rearrange, reconstruct and re-member. With time, patience, and practice (we'll do some exercises) you'll find the voice that calls out from every room the body houses. That voice is full of truth and feeling. It is not your father's, your mother's, or your teacher's voice—it is *yours*.

INTRODUCTION:
DESCENDING INTO
THE BODY

*After much thought, I realized that the trouble I had writing
that bleak Friday afternoon was due to my approach. I was
trying to analyze ... trying to explain rationally ... I was
failing miserably because I was approaching the task
through my head ... I had to drop into my belly.*

—Marion Woodman
Interview, *Common Boundary*
July 1992

*Yet if I were asked to name the most important items in a
writer's makeup, the things that shape his material and rush
him along the road to where he wants to go, I could only
warn him to look to his zest, see to his gusto.*

—Ray Bradbury
Zen in the Art of Writing

The call to write is a call that's received in the *body first*. For
hundreds of years poets and writers have described the creative
process as a *physical* urgency, a sense that things will fly apart
if they don't get the pencil to the page in time. Creativity is
not tidy or polite—it's *insistent*. It calls us to feel, not dimly,
not safely, but wildly, passionately, in every cell and fiber.

If we are to answer that call, we have to be able to *feel*
every part of our lives. A writer can't afford to walk numbly
through the house with a blanket over the head. When the
lover steps, dripping, from the shower and bends to dry herself,

1

the writer's eye takes in the droplets as they fall to the floor, and the fire of creativity is ignited: the little spheres of light encased in the water, the gently sloping curve from hairline to ankle, her hands as they guide the cloth over her skin. Let others drink life from a tiny cup! Face plunged in this ocean, the writer reaches deeply with every pore, not just to taste, but to merge with that greater Body, to experience the larger Self. To live like that, and to write from that truth, we have to radically reclaim and renew the body.

The Persian poet Kabir invites us to seriously consider the task:

> *Be strong then, and enter into your own body;*
> *there you have a solid place for your feet.*
> *Think about it carefully!*
> *Don't go off somewhere else!*
> *Kabir says this: just throw away all thoughts of*
> *   imaginary things,*
> *and stand firm in that which you are.*

—Kabir
from "#14" in *The Kabir Book*
translated by Robert Bly

Think of "standing on your own two feet." These words call up strength and trust that the ground beneath us will remain firm. We sense the body's independence, as well as its need for a good foundation.

Think of your skeleton, its solid resolve, the sturdy collection of bones that anchors your standing, walking, running, and resting. Every piece of writing—whether it seeks to inhabit a form or labors to tear apart the familiar—begins and proceeds from the physical structure we so often ignore. To write from the body, we become aware of our own inherent arrangement, as well as the "box" or "net" we have in mind to contain our words. We must learn to appreciate the body's sculptural elegance as well as its intricate circuitry. This way we come to rely on its obvious wisdom to arrange what we want to say.

It's not just our writing that will flourish once we return to the body. Our relationships take on a new fascination, a new sense of the unexpected. We watch through the moments of the day, understanding that they're richly pregnant and may give birth at any time. To return to the body is to begin to *live* creatively, and to carry that enthusiasm into our writing, as well as into our ballplaying, our cooking, our lovemaking, and our waking up in the morning.

To write from the body we must first *accept* our bodies, and before we do that, we have to come out of denial about how much we rely on our brains. When we brainstorm through our lives without much regard for our physical selves, debris is inevitably scattered in our path.

We started out as mystical thinkers in childhood, but many of us ended up using the mind as a means of escape from the world's vicissitudes. We concocted a dream world, or armed ourselves with rationalizations, in an attempt to explain to ourselves things that didn't make sense. Many of us had to contend with spoken and unspoken suggestions that we weren't supposed to act like children. We were supposed to stop crying on command. We were to grow up quickly, be nice, be good. We were told, dismissively, that the monsters in our bedrooms didn't exist. From this cacophony of unreasonable demands, one clear message rang out: "Don't listen to your *body*—listen to *me*!" What could we do? Where could we go?

We could seek refuge in our heads.

The same thing happened at school. We sat in straight rows of chairs (in my school, the chairs were bolted to the floor!) and we learned The Rules. Some of us even received lower learning from the "*board* of education," and by age thirteen or fourteen had shut down our bodies so completely that we'd turn and laugh at the one who was paddling us. By then we were giving *ourselves* weird messages: "I'm proving my strength by cutting off my feelings."

For most of us, physical movement was relegated to gym, where we were taunted, teased, and popped with wet towels.

The whole educational system of the time, both secular and religious, was at pains to deliver us from our own "primitive" impulses, the natural rhythms and needs of our bodies. The act of lovemaking was spoken about in whispers, or as a competition sport, or was openly reviled, depending on who was doing the talking. Only the brain and the spirit were to be worshipped, elevated, and educated, while the body's wild energies were left to wither. From the beginning it was a hopeless task. Where did our brain and spirit exist, if not in the body? And how could we hope to learn anything if *all* our selves—the muscle, the mind, the mystic—were not working together as equals?

We all know the rest of this story of imbalance: our beautiful physical being, and our vibrant, leaping energies huddled in the background as our brains conducted us to excellence, achievement, and early heart attacks. "I think, therefore I am" became our battle cry. We said it to ourselves as we slumped, exhausted, in our chairs at the end of the day.

When I ask people in my Writing from the Body workshops, "How do you *feel?*" the answer is, "I don't know, I've never really *thought* about it." We want to say and to write what we feel, but we've cut ourselves off from our bodies so completely that we've forgotten what feelings feel like! We can't think our way to our feelings any more than we can leap a stream without legs. When the people we love ask us to tell how we feel, too often we end up expounding on what we *think.*

THE BODY KNEW

Long before there were words
long before there was patience
the body was twiddling its thumbs

Long before this haze of lies this
swirl of stupid things
said and done
the body knew

Long before the animals ran
from men before the lands
were named before the clouds
rose up and flew
the body knew

The body knew the tongue
would come up with something to say
that the ears would listen that
the words would come like ants
that soon the brain would be
infested and the head would grow
hard and heavy
The body knew the body

would be forgotten
The body knew the body
would be used to take the brain
here and there to make
money *to make* relationships
to assume the countless postures
of idiocy—to sign the contracts
and treaties to stock the stores
the homes the schools the offices
the streets the prisons the battlefields
the body-bags the body knew

it would be lost
under fabrics that soon the belly would
hang and the back would be stiff
that the days would pass the months would

pass the years would pass
The body knew

it would be rated "X"
because the body knew words
would be used to deceive to
decorate to pack the space between bodies until
reaching out meant climbing the mountains
of things said
The body knew

the brain would be a bully
that the face would be a canvas forever
painted with words that love *could never be*
what they said it was   that a word
was always a mask
The body knew the body

would dream of headlessness the way
a breast dreams of bra-lessness of blouselessness
of sunlight and weightlessness
The body knew that someday
it would have to move to forget to
dance to forget that it knew
what it knew
that it knew

—Tim Seibles

So we'll begin with a descent into the body. We can follow the example of Natalie Goldberg (author of *Writing Down the Bones*), who says, "After all my years of Western education, I wanted to learn how not to think." Teaching the mind to settle down is absolutely necessary to our task.

Learning not to think takes time, courage, and effort. Of course, we're not going to exile our mentality the way we've done to our emotions. But we can insist that every part of us be given its proper place, especially when we're involved in creating, and in sharing our most authentic Self with the people we love. The brain, while capable of handling a remarkable number of tasks at once, is still secondary in this enterprise. It is the *servant* of creativity, not the master. There is an ancient thrill of wisdom lying dormant *in our bodies*. Somewhere in there, we know how to get through the high grass without being devoured by lions. Long before conception occurs, a woman's body knows how to give birth to her child. The body harbors all this essential knowledge, and more. If given its rightful place in our lives, it will not only serve and protect us, it will support and guide the intellect in artful harmony. And from that harmony our very best writing—our art, in *all* its forms—will become manifest.

Scientists say that we're only accessing about three percent of the brain's total capacity. What more might the brain be capable of, if we took the body out of its chains and let the two play together? We know that three percent isn't enough to help us attend to our children or empathize with our lover's pain. When we place the pen to the page, we certainly want to communicate more than three percent of our sorrows and joys to the world. If we are to live with passionate conviction, more of the remaining ninety-seven percent must be released. We do this by freeing the energy, memory, and magic that are stored throughout the body.

To repress the impulses of our nature requires a tremendous exertion of physical energy. It isn't easy to hold back the true Self and still hold one's head high. Whatever forces we have expended in this effort are not available for creative acts. When we begin to understand this, we're ready to rebel, to descend into the body's untold stories. More often than not, we must venture into the past to release them.

Releasing pent-up emotions not only frees energy, it cleanses and clarifies our thinking. One of my favorite writers, Robert A. Johnson (Jungian analyst and author of wonderful books such as *He* and *She*), gives testimony to the power of consulting the body's energies before giving a talk to a group:

> A wise woman once showed me how to get more energy when I complained that I was exhausted before lecturing. She instructed me to go to a private room just before the talk, take a towel, dampen it so it would be very heavy, then throw the towel, wrapped up in a ball, at the floor as hard as I could— and shout. I felt infinitely foolish doing this, for it is not my style. But when I walked out to the lecture platform after such an exercise there was fire in my eyes. I had energy, stamina and "Voice."
>
> —from *Owning Your Own Shadow*

In other words, Energy equals Voice. The body must be recognized, "re-membered" and recharged. The energy we've been using to repress and forget must be channeled differently if we want a dynamic contact between ourselves and others. Once we are experiencing that contact our writing will come from us, as John Keats said, "as naturally as leaves to a tree, or it had best not come at all."

You are about to begin to read, feel, and think with your whole body. To kindle our inspiration, we will look to the poetry and prose of other writers. I have drawn heavily from the world of poetry here, because poetry is what sparked *my* descent into the body. Poetry was my first love, and helped me move back down South into my own body, after having spent so much time in the chilly North of the mind. Poetry is the energy of language in its purest form, thought and feeling distilled to their essence. If you are biased against poetry or have little experience reading it, I hope you'll put that bias aside to find out what poetry can do and where it can take you.

Poetry is often hidden in all manner of prose: the business letter, the essay, the novel. In China, to be assigned a government post, the prospective civil servant must be able not only to recite verse, but to write it as well. In our own culture we are constantly encouraged to ascend—to look up, to move up, and to think lofty thoughts. The poetry presented here (along with a number of selections from novels and plays) will take you *deep down* into the rhythms of your body and soul. If you use the poems as suggested, they can release in you new energies that will charge your words with power and grace.

FREEING UP THE ENERGY TO WRITE

Energy creates energy.

—Albert Einstein

DANSE RUSSE

When my wife is sleeping
and the baby and Kathleen
are sleeping
and the sun is a flame-white disc
in silken mists
above shining trees,—
if I in my north room
dance naked, grotesquely
before my mirror
waving my shirt around my head
and singing softly to myself:
"I am lonely, lonely.
I was born to be lonely,
I am best so!"
If I admire my arms, my face,

my shoulders, flanks, buttocks
against the yellow drawn shades,—
who shall say I am not
the happy genius of my household?

—William Carlos Williams

If you did not write every day, the poisons would accumulate and you would begin to die, or act crazy or both—you must stay drunk on writing so reality cannot destroy you.

—Ray Bradbury
  The Zen in the Art of Writing

As children, we had lots of energy and were constantly creating. We told our friends incredible tales and built kingdoms for our adventures. We flew with angels and fled from trolls. Language was a constantly available toy: we invented songs and rhymes to repeat to ourselves. In describing this time in his own childhood, Dylan Thomas said,

> I did not care what the words said, nor what happened to Jack and Jill and Mother Goose and the rest of them; I cared for the shapes of sound that their names, and the words describing their actions, made in my ears; I cared for the colours the words cast on my eyes.

As children, we played freely with sound and expression. But somewhere along the way we began editing what came naturally to us. We heard others tell their stories differently; we noticed the praise they got. Or we watched stories played out on television and concluded that they were more exciting than what we had made up on our own. Gradually, subtly, we began to hold things in, instead of turning them loose into the world. And our precious energy went the way of the kingdoms, and the angels. The trolls stayed on; they just changed form—

appearing as anger, sadness, guilt, frustration, fear. These trolls went into our bodies to hide, and all the criticisms we heard and believed about ourselves marched in right behind them.

We want to become as free to create as we were in childhood. We know that what we have to tell is unique, unlike what anyone else would reveal. To do this, we must be willing to give voice to the dusty collection of disappointments and anxieties that crowd our inner territory.

So much of creativity is an attempt to retranslate the most closely guarded stories of our lives. The insistent archaeologist within us demands that we detect our own tension, stress, and distress and trace them back to their origins. As Marion Woodman observes, "Powerful energies are locked in our bodies." If we do not discharge the pressures stored in our muscles and tissues, in our backs, our faces, throats, and bellies, in our arms and legs, then the energy gets stuck. When we don't release these tensions, we often end up in a breathless effort to talk them out or write them out, when it would have been easier to stretch, sigh, shout, pound, punch, or dance them out in the beginning.

What does all this have to do with writing? Until I discovered the wealth of energies—disguised as ancient angers, griefs, sorrows, rages, and joys—rumbling around in my frozen body, I couldn't write what I wanted to write. I couldn't speak my own truth. Again and again I hid from myself and others, trying to get others to listen to me when I hadn't yet listened within, wanting others to understand my passions when I scarcely knew what they were. For decades, I had been trying to "talk things out," and it wasn't working.

Have you ever had an epic talk with a friend or lover, when you tried to *talk* through the layers of meaning you knew were hidden somewhere in the details of your relationship? After an hour or two of this, have you ever felt that you still hadn't said what you started out to say? In the same way, as writers we often speak from our confusion rather than from our certainty, our conviction. We try to write out pounds of pain and acres of interrupted dreams, but we don't come up with anything that excites or moves us because writing, like talking, cannot adequately discharge all that unexpressed physical energy. And, perhaps more importantly, we cannot write *well* until we free up the energy to write.

We will use body writing exercises to get to our deeply hidden stories. Doing this, we give a long-deserved attention to ourselves. What happens when we begin to listen to the stories and poems that wait within us to be discovered, when we stop laboring to "make things up"? The mind clears, the body relaxes, the prison bars fall away. Then we read with excitement our own passionate dreams, and the wisdom of our years.

If we want to write the kind of stuff that Emily Dickinson says "takes the top of my head off," we have to go to the body's closet, pry open the door, let the shouts and yelps fly, and welcome the skeletons that come clattering out. "We try to push all the parts of ourselves we don't like into our bodies," says Marion Woodman. We also push into our bodies all the mean and thoughtless things that others ever said to us. We've made the body a dumping ground for the toxic waste of our past—the judgments, the angry insults, the jealousies. The color of our passions, positive or negative, remains hidden, both in our writing and in the rest of our life.

Gabrielle Lusser Rico says, ". . . most of us have learned to write, not in a state of release, but by rule, with the result generally being flat, dull, turgid—most certainly not original, natural, free." Like our writing, we stay flat and dull, unable to say what comes freely, as long as we hold on to the junkyard of the past as though it were a storehouse of precious artifacts. But here's the good news: the energy we had, we still have. When we learn to free that energy, we'll find that our imagination still knows how to soar.

Ours is a simple agenda: to tell the truth. When we do,

"we bring up living words like fishes hooked in their gills, leaping from the deep," says the thirteenth-century poet Lu Chi. When we go against our impulses, our language grows unclear, reflecting the mind's preoccupation with obscuring the passions and pains that make us human. As Lu Chi explains, "One whose language remains muddled cannot do it; only when held in a clear mind can the language become noble." To ensure that our language is honorable and our writing worthwhile, we ourselves must become noble. And to do that requires honest courage.

Find a place and time where you won't be disturbed. Spend about fifteen minutes thinking *and feeling* what you would like to say about some event in the past. It could be something that happened in the recent past or in your youth or childhood. Before you attempt to write it out, try shouting it out in as few words as you possibly can. If you're in an apartment with thin walls, or in some other situation where you don't want to be heard, you can muffle your shouts with a thick pillow. This way you'll get a similar, although not as poignant, effect. At some point, if you continue to practice this, then just as Robert Johnson did with his wet towel, you will experience a release, and next a rush of energy. When you reach that point, write about the memory. If you see that your thinking is not yet clear—that is, if the words seem "muddled"—go back and repeat the exercise until you break through that barrier. Most of us have stored up shouts and screams that we would have let go of decades ago, social weather permitting. When you've written down something that feels clear to you, put it away for a while. Let it sit. In a few days, it will look entirely different. You may want to add to it; you may feel like chucking it. The most important thing is, you're engaged in the practice of writing.

This exercise will work best if you record the instructions onto audiotape, then play it back while you follow along. This way your body is free to focus solely on the experience.

You'll need some upbeat music, light and fast. Find a place and time where you won't be disturbed. Standing up straight, begin to march in place to the music. Be very deliberate about feeling each foot as it hits the ground. Closing your eyes, sink deep into the experience of marching in place. Take your awareness into your legs, your thighs, your calves, your feet, deep into the ground. Now open your eyes. Loosen your legs: shake them around. Let your legs get jazzy now—wiggling your toes, your fingers, your eyes, your hips, your elbows, your head. Now let all of these wiggling parts of you drop slowly and gently to the ground, or to a chair. Sit softly. Close your eyes and let the weight of your arms stretch them out. Now feel your arms growing longer and longer. Reach with your arms all the way out of the room, all the way out of town, until you touch something very far away. What is it? Feel everything about whatever it is: its color, its texture, its smell, the sound it makes. There are no rules. Now bring your arms back to their normal size, nearer your body. Cross your arms in front and hug your shoulders. Now, write about your experience quickly. Don't stop for anything—it will only be the Inner Critic, come to disturb the flow. Just keep going until you're finished. For now, don't judge what you've written. It's only a souvenir.

I'm always pleasantly surprised to see how easy it is to come up with new material for writing simply by engaging in an exercise that takes me back into my body. If you had good results with one or both of the exercises above, consider making such exercises a part of your discipline as a writer. You probably don't need to start *every* writing session with an exercise, but by doing this even occasionally, you are trusting your body to enliven your work.

WRITER'S BLOCK BEGINS IN THE BODY

My question is "When did other people give up the idea of being a poet?" You know when we are kids we make up things, we write, and for me the puzzle is not that some people are still writing, the real question is why did the other people stop?

—William Stafford

The repressed cannot exist. The buried is kept below. The block obstructs the passageway prohibiting speech.

—Bonnie Friedman
Writing Past Dark

Most would-be writers have several blocks that keep them from writing or creating. I'm not referring to "writer's block" as we ordinarily think of it, but to actual physical blockages in the body that prevent us from writing our truth.

Like most children, I was in love with words and stories by the age of two, but at some point I lost this innate longing for language. I saw that little boys were to be seen and not heard, that big boys don't express a wide range of emotions, and that tough guys speak very little and hold in a lot. I also learned that if I overtly loved language and literature, art and music, I would be considered a little weird—my sexuality might even be called into question. All this led me to conclude that a "real man" shouldn't talk much, and therefore shouldn't become a writer. Many girls received a similar, albeit unspoken, message that creative writing was a waste of time, that it wasn't "productive." Math, science, biology, law, accounting, engineering—these were worthy pursuits. Never mind that the foundation of all these disciplines lay in the writings of creative minds, and often of expansively dreaming souls. Somehow that crucial fact had been lost.

There were the subtler negative messages, and there were those that were not so subtle. We heard, "You're too sensitive," "You're a daydreamer," "Wake up and live in the real world." "Marry and have kids, and *after they're grown you can start to create*" (quite a contradiction in terms). These words went straight into our bodies. In junior high, high school, and college we heard more: "You don't have a strong aptitude for language," or "Writers are rare, gifted people." The implication, of course, was that we were not gifted. So we exiled ourselves to a kind of writer's hell where many of us have languished in silence ever since.

Such destructive messages take the physical form of stress and tension that lodges in our throats, our backs, and our bones. When we pick up a pen to write down a few thoughts, those messages seize us like a cold hand. Too often we surrender too easily: we drop the pen (or walk away from the computer) convinced that "they were right."

If you are to reveal the truth that is within you, these blocks must be removed. The energy of your anger, grief, and frustration must be discharged, to make room for the natural process of creation. Talking it out with someone you trust is a good form of release, as far as it goes. But if after a good, long talk your body is still clamoring for its say, you must get up and move around to free those energies and break through the blocks. That is the aim of this book, and that's what we're going to do together. But first it's important to understand fully why and how this "breaking through" will help your writing become what it was meant to be.

By breaking free from the energy blocks we've been carrying, we come closer to our ultimate goal: to push beyond our physical limitations. Not to leave the body—that's dissociation—but to go so far into the body that we write from the totality of who we are and always have been. By embracing the body at depth, we so fully inhabit it that the ego relaxes its stranglehold and only the writing remains, jotting itself onto the page like rain falling into a river.

To embrace our body's truth is to embrace our past. There is no other way. The body is home to all that has happened to us, and it remembers. Fortunately, if we will engage in the process of remembering with full vigor, great riches emerge. In his breakthrough book, *The Poetics of Reverie,* Gaston Bachelard writes,

> . . . in waking life, . . . when reverie works on our history, the childhood which is within us brings us its benefits. One needs . . . to live with the child he has been. From such living he achieves a consciousness of roots, and the entire tree of his being takes comfort from it.

Not everything we discover in ourselves will be *comfortable.* But we need to know the truth of our roots if we are to write from that depth. Our roots don't have to be pleasant to be comforting. Just the act of claiming our own history, of pledging ourselves to its truth, provides peace of mind. It also feeds our writing—we must know our whole story before we can tell it.

One of the most persistent messages I received growing up was that I wasn't very smart. The atmosphere was so tense at home that my thinking often was not clear, and this in itself raised further doubts about my intellectual abilities.

I didn't learn quickly, particularly mechanical skills, and math was extremely difficult for me. Over time I developed the sincere feeling that I just wasn't very bright. Until I was thirty-three years old, I secretly suspected that I was slightly developmentally disabled. Never mind that I had three bachelor's degrees and a master's, was working on a Ph.D., and had taught at a university for six years.

I was raised in the South by parents who were barely literate. In the 1940s and 1950s such folks were referred to as "hillbillies." I was ashamed of my origins; I thought one had to have been born north of the Mason-Dixon line to be able to write—ideally, from New York or Massachusetts. But Alabama? So I wanted to write a dissertation to prove that even people from Alabama had brains—maybe not in excess, but in adequate proportion to the rest of the nation's people. And even though I had read and studied most of the great southern writers, I assumed that they had each emigrated to New York at some point, to make their mark on the literary world.

That's a part of my story. You have your own. You have your own messages. What were they? Who spoke them? What did you feel like when you heard them? How do you feel about those messages, and the messengers, now? Before writing your answer: get up, walk, run, swing your arms like a dancer, shadowbox like a contender, and let out any sounds or sighs that want to come out of you. Acknowledge how much it has cost you to carry these messages in your muscle and bone, in your thought and feeling.

Now write a story, a poem, a one-act play, or a letter. Write how you feel about those destructive messages. Tell the whole truth at last. If fears arise, name them and you will dissipate their power. We don't have to go on fighting our fear, telling ourselves, "Everything's fine." As we write from the body, we touch the center of ourselves. In doing so we discover to our surprise that everything truly *is* fine, and that a part of us remains safe regardless of what happens to us in the world.

My truth is this: I wasn't disabled. But I did become tense and scared when unreasonable demands were placed on me.

Write your own truth boldly, loudly. Stay close to the body's sounds, to its rhythms of breath and bone, and *they* will tell you what to write.

Take out a few sheets of paper and tear them into three or four fairly equal strips. Now pick up a strip and write down one of the negative messages you received that prevents you from writing or creating. ("I don't know how to write," "I'm not talented," "Other people won't like what I write.") Wad it into a ball and throw it. Write down another message, and another, and another. Keep wadding them up and throwing them down. Let yourself enjoy the throwing! A variation: take a whole sheet of paper and write the message in big block letters. Fold the page into an airplane and let it fly! Now grab it and wad it up. Tear it up if you like. Get a trash can and a long strip of masking tape. Use the masking tape to make a sign for the trash can: LIES. Tape it on, and then go hunting. Look around until you've found all the little wadded-up lies, and shoot them into the trash can. Feel the finality of disposing of the lies. If you like, you can carry them to a safe spot and burn them in a ritual fire. You can sing a song of goodbye. When this is done, take some time to sit quietly, and close your eyes. Notice the quality of your breathing. Deep inside yourself, watch what it feels like to be free of lies.

INSPIRATION:
THE BREATH
AND THE
WORD

*Because I felt betrayed by my body, as I grew older I
continued to dissociate myself from it . . . To my way of
thinking, the life of the head was surely to be preferred to the
life of the body . . . I had so little bodily awareness that I did
not realize that, by cutting off my breathing, I was also
cutting myself off from my sensations and feelings.*

—Kate Dawson
Leaving My Father's House

The Spanish poet Federico García Lorca once explained that
all true art must be produced out of the "energetic instinct"
that Spaniards refer to as the *duende*, "the mystery, the roots
that probe through the mire that we all know of and do not
understand." In his essay on the *duende*, Lorca paints in a
number of ways the necessity of the artist's intimacy with the
Shadow Self, the "black sounds" that our words carry when,
as writers, we have touched our own darkness and reemerged
vulnerably awake, humbled, and even more alive.

We must fully reclaim the breath, because without it the
body withers and so does our writing. The message written by

the tight chest, the stilted body, carries no *duende*, no darkness, no belly stretched wide by the breath. Such writing is a mere whistle. It rises up like a ghost, substanceless, with a mask for a face, and we do not believe it.

What must we do to reclaim the body, the breath? We must address the fear that paralyzes us, the darknesses we have held back like stifled coughs and whispers. We must open ourselves, allowing the wind to enter and change us.

Imagine you are going to the page right now, with the thought "I'm going to write something." You may even want to go directly to your desk and sit in front of the blank page with pen in hand, to embrace the full experience of beginning to write. When you did this, what happened to your breath? Did you find yourself breathing deeply, the full and even rhythm of your inspiration moving naturally through you? Or did you tighten up, making shallow inhalations, perhaps even holding your breath?

When we human beings are scared, excited, hurried, or anxious, we stop breathing. The sight and sound of a distressing scene, or the momentary flicker of a past trauma, causes us to hold our breath. Shallow breathing is a way of stopping short, of postponing full involvement in whatever is going on. By shutting down our air supply, we can alter our consciousness. We begin to feel lightheaded, our eyes glaze over, and our emotions recede into the distance. They *recede*; they don't disappear. To begin writing with the full power of our body's knowledge, we must welcome our life, our breath, and our emotions completely. We have only to begin breathing fully to show Life that we are serious about embracing her.

When we breathe deeply, we more completely inhabit our bodies, and, yes, our pains, but also our contentment and our ecstasy. Unfortunately, we have made a habit of cutting off the breath in midstream. We allow our bodies just enough oxygen to keep the brain going, the vital functions operating at half-mast. But it's not enough air for us to *feel* this intricate, magnificent life.

"I'm ready," you say. "I'm certainly willing to take deeper breaths, if it will bring my novel into being!" But once we begin embracing the breath, an inner battle ensues. The mind comes up with platitudes it has used for years to keep us in limbo: "There, now. Don't be silly. It's not that bad. It doesn't really hurt. Crying won't help. It's water under the bridge, spilt milk, stiff upper lip, pull yourself together." What the mind is really saying is "Don't feel. Forget it. We don't have time for this. Get back to work!" These messages have had us by the throat for so long that we've forgotten we're in danger.

But also in childhood, now and then a comforting voice would offer real wisdom: "Slow down for a moment. Take a deep breath. What is it you want to tell me? Let's count to ten and start over." People who were *breathing their lives* not only encouraged us to take deep breaths, but showed us how to do it. They invited the air in with their whole bodies, and so could listen with their full attention as we poured out our wild stories, our childhood worries and secret mistakes. By breathing fully, these listeners allowed our pain to pass out of us. They didn't absorb our pain; they only listened with respect. I try to practice this when I do emotional release work in workshops. When I take full, deep breaths while someone else is experiencing wave upon wave of grief, I'm communicating that I not only encourage and welcome what that person is feeling, but also that my own body will survive the process intact. In our search for mentors, we must bear in mind that we need the support of people who *live* in their bodies, who aren't just visitors in their own skins.

Intimately following the natural movement of our own breath and speech while writing causes our inspiration to take fresh and unexpected forms. Sometimes when I feel bored with my writing, I take a break to pick up a novel or a book of poems by a favorite author. So often, after absorbing the rhythmic particularities of someone else's writing for a while, I return to my own work with new fervor, new lines and phrases busily composing themselves. If I stay focused, close to my breath, I know I will hook those fish—they won't get away.

By following the breath instead of always being led by the brain, you'll find yourself in places you didn't "think" you'd ever visit. Going into these unknown places is motivation to write; indeed, it's the payoff. By breathing into your writing, descending into the body and its past, you will be able to see and report parts of your experience that were previously hidden from you.

In my workshop not long ago, I met Malcolm, an accomplished editor for a local newspaper. As part of our work together, I asked him to direct his attention to his breath. He began telling how his writing was unsatisfying to him, and that he was sure it had to do with his job—always reading someone else's prose. After listening to him for four or five minutes I asked him to become still and focus his attention solely on his breath. Then I asked Malcolm to take pen and paper and, along with each exhalation, write the words or phrases that spontaneously arose. At first he wrote single words: "anger," "time," "talent," and "touch." Then I asked him to write at least one or two sentences as fast as he could, without stopping at all to think. Here is what Malcolm wrote:

> By the time my father was ten years younger than I
> am the light in his eyes had disappeared. Dad was
> afraid to touch me, and touch the talent that he saw
> in me but could not see in himself.

Malcolm worked these two sentences into a short story. In the process of "breathing through" that story, he found a windstorm of emotions buried deep in his chest. When he had finished the story, Malcolm looked up and said, "God, I didn't know that was in there."

Try reading the following poem out loud. Notice the movement of your breath as you read these lines:

THE STILL TIME

I know there is still time—
time for the hands
to open, for the bones of them
to be filled
by those failed harvests of want,
the bread imagined of the days of not having.

Now that the fear
has been rummaged down to its husk,
and the wind blowing
the flesh away translates itself
into flesh and the flesh
streams in its reveries on the wind.

I remember those summer nights
when I was young and empty,
when I lay through the darkness
wanting, wanting,
knowing
I would have nothing of anything I
    wanted—
that total craving
that hollows the heart out irreversibly.

So it surprises me now to hear
the steps of my life following me—
so much of it gone
it returns, everything that drove me crazy
comes back, blessing the misery
of each step it took me into the world;

as though prayer had ended
and the changed
air between the palms goes free
to become the glitter
on common things that inexplicably shine.

And all the old voices,
which once made broken-off, choked, parrot-
    incoherences,
speak again,
this time on the palatum cordis, all of them
saying there is time, still time,
for those who can groan
to sing,
for those who can sing to heal themselves.

—Galway Kinnell

Exercise: Take out a pen and paper. Using Kinnell's poem as inspiration, begin taking full, deep breaths, letting the air stretch out your diaphragm. Then write down the words "When I was young and empty." Put down your pen and again breathe fully and deeply for a few moments. Write whatever bursts forth from the breath. Let the pen follow where the breath leads.

Now observe the movement of air through your lungs as you read (aloud) this passage from the Prologue to Ralph Ellison's *Invisible Man*:

I am an invisible man. No, I am not a spook like those who haunted Edgar Allan Poe; nor am I one of your Hollywood-movie ectoplasms. I am a man of substance, of flesh and bone, fiber and liquids—and I might even be said to possess a mind. I am invisible, understand, simply because people refuse to see me. Like the bodiless heads you see sometimes in circus sideshows, it is as though I have been surrounded

by mirrors of hard, distorting glass. When they approach me they see only my surroundings, themselves, or figments of their imagination—indeed,
anything and everything except me.

This passage begins one of the most poignantly written novels
ever to illustrate racism and its psychological and spiritual
effects. Although the story uses the analogy of disembodiment
to show the effects of racism, the movement of breath in the
passage is free and open, firmly anchored to the body.

Exercise: As you reread aloud the following sentence from
Ellison's Prologue, take deep, slow breaths between each word:
I ... *breath* ... am ... *breath* ... invisible, ... *breath* ... understand, ... *breath* ... simply ... *breath* ... because ... *breath* ...
people ... *breath* ... refuse ... *breath* ... to see ... *breath* ...
me.

Now pick up your pen and write the first thing that comes
across your mental screen, as you continue to breathe deeply
and slowly. With each word that goes onto the page, paint your
Self on this blank canvas.

Everything we write comes from what we are, from what
we have inside. If we commit to inhabiting our bodies completely, our writing will be the poetry or prose of transformation, and it will carry in it the power of this insistent inner
movement. In his "Projective Verse," Charles Olson writes, "A
poem is energy transferred from where the poet got it." If the
energy we hold is the energy of fear, of anxiety, of grief and
suffering, then that is what will form itself into a poem (or
prose) on the page. That fear or grief will exist as a rhythmic
undercurrent in the voice of the work, if not in its immediate
content.

When we allow that inspiration to break up the debris of
stored feelings, letting them wash over and through us and on
downstream, then the stream is cleared and cleansed. Then a
new face and voice, born of a different energy, will become

evident in our written creations. Our words will carry the energy of initiation, for we will have been through the fire of an ordeal in making them.

I challenge you to bring full-bodied breathing into all parts of your life: walking, eating, lovemaking, cooking, writing, work. When you write, let your feelings spill onto the page. If you don't like this part of the writing, you can cut it later. But in the first flush of creation, don't let anything stop the breath or the pen.

Let your words ebb and flow along with the body's necessary weather. I imagine James Joyce writing *Ulysses* this way, especially the following favorite passage, right at the end of the novel:

> . . . and then I asked him with my eyes to ask again yes and then he asked me would I yes to say yes my mountain flower and first I put my arms around him yes and drew him down to me so he could feel my breasts all perfume yes and his heart was going like mad and yes I said yes I will Yes.

The breath in this writing is quick and immediate, true to the passion it describes.

We've all read words that were "uninspired," literally lacking breath. Such writing, whatever its form, cannot sustain us. To find our truth, we must be willing to go under: to dive deep into ourselves and come up gasping, clutching something precious in the fist. We may be able to "invent" phrases that give brief entertainment to the brain, but these are never memorable, because they do not answer our perpetual longing.

The following two exercises will work best for you if you either have someone else read the instructions to you as you do the exercise or record the instructions on audiotape so that you can play them back while you do the exercise. This way you can give your undivided attention to the experience.

An exercise for awakening the creativity inherent in the breath: Become still and quiet, in a place where you will not be disturbed. Closing your eyes, focusing on the movement of your breath. Imagine breathing in the coolness of the ocean, its whitenesses, its darknesses, its ebb and flow. Imagine you are breathing in multicolored fish, one by one. As you breathe in, they swim into your body. As you breathe out, they swim away from you.

Breathe in. . . . Breathe out. . . . Breathe in. . . . Now breathe out the entire ocean in one huge gushing wave. Send the ocean far into the distance.

Imagine a blazing bonfire. Breathe in that fire. Hear the crackling in your chest as you inhale the wildly leaping flames. Watch the fire grow within you. Each time you breathe in, the fire rises higher. When you breathe out, the fire dies down. Now breathe the fire up to its greatest height. Feel its largeness, its heat and its power. Now breathe out long, and let the fire go out along with the breath. Watch the fire dwindle to a few red coals. Keep breathing quietly in and out. See that only ashes are left. Coming back to where you are, taking a deep breath in, and a deep breath out. Rest a few moments, then begin breath-writing: With each breath in, gather your strength, and as you breathe out, place your pen to the paper and write whatever comes from the pen.

> Do not think that *you* are writing. Let the pen, the hand, and the arm write. Above all, let the breath write. When you need to breathe in, stop writing. As you exhale, let the writing begin again. Write as long as you need to. When the page is filled, read with respect what your body and your breath have written there.

The experience of our original truth and creativity is what we most long for in our lives. We search for it everywhere: in the events we see and hear, in the words and acts of others, and in the words we read and write. Whenever I'm selecting writings to include in a reading or workshop, I choose only those that carry the power and rhythm of the breath. I can know these writings by the goosebumps I get every time I read them.

THE LONGING

What often passes for depression in writers, in artists of all kinds, is actually the longing for union, for the merging we experience in the moment of creating. Of course, this longing is evidence of our larger search—for our greater Self and for the complete fulfillment, the bliss, of that supreme experience.

IN A DARK TIME

In a dark time, the eye begins to see,
I meet my shadow in the deepening shade;
I hear my echo in the echoing wood—

A lord of nature weeping to a tree.
I live between the heron and the wren,
Beast of the hill and serpents of the den.

What's madness but nobility of soul
At odds with circumstance? The day's on fire!
I know the purity of pure despair,
My shadow pinned against a sweating wall.
That place among the rocks—is it a cave,
Or winding path? The edge is what I have.

A steady storm of correspondences!
A night flowing with birds, a ragged moon,
And in broad day the midnight come again!
A man goes far to find out what he is—
Death of the self in a long, tearless night,
All natural shapes blazing unnatural light.

Dark, dark my light, and darker my desire.
My soul, like some heat-maddened summer fly,
Keeps buzzing at the sill. Which I is I?
A fallen man, I climb out of my fear.
The mind enters itself, and God the mind.
And one is One, free in the tearing wind.

—Theodore Roethke

Given that I have now almost successfully navigated through the shoals of Midlife, I can say with conviction that I have known and felt Roethke's words all through my body. From the age of thirty-three to forty-three I feel I have been "pinned to a sweating wall," and that a "tearing wind" was blowing through my chest cavity on its way through Central Texas.

Depression is quite real for many people. Millions of dollars are spent annually to relieve us of its debilitating consequences. Over the years I have come to believe that a good deal of this depression is due to an inability to feel our emotions. There is an inner need to feel our lives deeply, but who would understand if we kicked up our heels in a jig down the sidewalk? When we feel ecstatic, in love, when we raise our faces to the sky in utter gratitude for this life, how is that joy expressed in the body? It isn't. We hold it in, just as we hold in our so-called negative emotions.

Writers need to feel. Otherwise, how will we sense the "trouble," the urgency that prods us to begin? We want to express our longing in its intensity. We need to write with a keen awareness of this longing, to know it better, for it is our greatest Self in seed form. What is the object of your longing? Every writer must find out an answer that will sustain, for not knowing your goal will stop your writing.

Take out a pen and paper and write the words "THIS LONGING" across the top of the page. Then list your longings. Here is a sample list I created in my last Writing from the Body workshop:

THIS LONGING

FOR: *Communication*

Childhood

Agreement

Being heard

Peace

Connection

Guidance

A *dance partner*

A *child*

Consciousness

These are some of the forms of longing that live in my body like bees in a hive. It's as though the hive's entrance has been blocked and word is spreading that the Queen is dead. Everywhere honey is dripping from the walls, and yet my longings keep my insides frenetically buzzing, too distracted to taste any sweetness. In the best writing, the depth of the longing *is* the sweetness. Notice how both satisfaction and yearning blend in this prose excerpt from the Introduction to *Neruda and Vallejo*, edited by Robert Bly:

> His love of life never falters. His love of women never falters. He loves them, the more unpredictable the better; he remembers Josie Bliss, who was so wild and nearly killed him twice with her knife; but when she went outside at morning to piss, the sound was like honey.

To get the bees out of their hive, use fire and smoke. Touch the Shadow, delve into what you'd rather not say, allow your breath to rise up wild within you and do not reject what it creates. From this apparent chaos, a hidden nectar flows.

Sometimes the smoke comes from the fire of our anger at having been told we can't write, or that our mind is unprepared, or that we should choose a vocation that pays the bills. Sometimes we're mad at our children for needing so much of our time, or at a partner who doesn't understand our passion for the written word. This anger often drives our feelings swarming out of us into the open. The flight of our fury lets us know that we don't have a "depressed" body or soul after all, but that we've only been stopping our longing. Every writer, at some point in life, must admit that this yearning is a part of everyday life, indeed is the lifeblood itself, and that depression comes when we try to stop the flood, when we do not act, do not create.

I long to write words that will fly out toward you like bees that cover our arms as together we scoop out the rich sweetness of what is said in the space between our words. I accept that I will never say all that must be said. I accept that I will be stung badly once or twice, because nothing of great value is ever gained for free.

The following poem will give you a further taste of what I mean. As you read it, hear each line as though it were speaking inside you, and breathe with the poem: inhale before you begin, and exhale as you speak, inhaling at the end of each line. Notice the relationship of the breath to the line breaks, how the poet uses the breath to achieve an impassioned, "breathless" effect.

WHAT THEY DO TO YOU IN DISTANT PLACES

I never told you.
There was a woman—in the greening season
of a tropical island
where I had gone to break some hard
    thoughts
across my knee
and also, although I am no athlete
but breathe with my stomach like the satyr
and live in my stomach
according to bile and acid and bread and
    bitter chocolate,
to run a long race for the first time.
On that morning,
it was raining in great screens
of the purest water and almost no one at 4
    a.m.
where I waited, half-sheltered
by the edge of my dark hotel, for a let-up.

Except her, suddenly
from nowhere—smelling of long hair and
*   dew,*
smelling of dew and grass and a little
*   powder.*
She wore a dress that moved.
She had been out dancing and the night and
*   she*
were young.
I wore a black watch cap like an old sailor
but I was all there was.

I said no, I had to do something else.
She asked how far? And
if I would run all that way—hours.
I said I'd try,
and then she kissed me for luck
and her mouth on mine was as sweet as the
*   wild guava*
and the smell of her hair
was that of the little bit of dew the lover
brings home from the park
when again she shows up in the morning.

I don't know where I have been
that I have ever had such a kiss
that asked nothing and gave everything.

I walked out into the rain
as if blessed. But I had forgotten
what they do to you in distant places,
taking away your memory
before sending you back. You and me.
I confess,
I forgot her within the hour
in the gross odors of my labors.

If I had known what she was doing. . . .
Perhaps she's with you now.

—Marvin Bell

Now read through this passage from the novel *Fried Green Tomatoes at the Whistle Stop Cafe*, by Fannie Flagg, keeping aware of the breath again. Notice the rhythms of concern, and of resignation, in the flow of these words:

> . . . as the train pulled away, he'd stepped on the track, tipped his hat, and flashed his lady killer smile at her; just as the whistle blew. They say he never even heard the train that was coming up behind him. Oh, how I wish to this day Cleo had never lent him that straw hat.
>
> She shook her head. "You just don't know, it like to have killed us all. But the one that took it hardest was Idgie. She must have been twelve or thirteen at the time, and had been over in Troutville playing ball when it happened. Cleo had to go over and get her.
>
> "You never saw anybody hurt so much. I thought she would die right along with him. It would break your heart to look at her. She ran away the day of the funeral. Just couldn't stand it. And when she did come home, all she did was go upstairs and sit in Buddy's room for hours on end, just sit up there in the dark. And when she couldn't bear to be home any longer, she'd just take off and go stay with Sipsey over in Troutville . . . but she never did cry. She was too hurt to cry. . . . You know, a heart can be broken, but it keeps on beating, just the same."

Woven throughout these sentences is the breath of conversation, the rhythm of storytelling, the immediacy of seeing the story as one speaks it. Giving over the writing to the body's natural movements brings into our work new content that we might have edited out, had we been "paying closer attention." To let the breath do the writing, we keep moving, allowing specific details to flow onto the page as they will. What would have happened if, after writing, "Oh, how I wish to this day Cleo had never lent him that straw hat," Fannie Flagg had stopped and allowed herself to think, "Wait a minute. What does the straw hat have to do with it?" As it stands, it is a fascinating conversational detail that conveys the narrator's powerless regret, and gives authenticity to our imagined experience of listening to a very elderly woman relating her story. If you will write along the stream of your breath, similar riches will arise in your writing.

The two pieces of work above produce a chill and a quiver in my body. If they don't give you goosebumps, then start your own search. Find writing that enlivens you, that ignites your own desire to write. When you find such writings, I encourage you to read them out loud, taking full breaths as you read. Doing this, allow yourself time and room to experience any emotions that may arise.

By seeking out influences, you expand the repertoire of song that inhabits your body's memory. When you read the work of great writers, you "borrow" their greatness by taking the rhythms of their language into your cells. This happens in much the same way that you pick up mannerisms and quirks of speech from your lover or spouse, and your dearest friends. By consciously putting yourself in the way of the masters, you will pick up new approaches to language. You will not be imitating; you will have *physically stored* the felt qualities of their writing. You need only refer to your own breath to make them manifest.

Breathing into our writing, we come to understand what Natalie Goldberg means when she says that "writing is not a performance but a generosity." With great excitement, we enter the forward movement of giving ourselves away.

Breath exercise: Sit quietly in a straight-backed chair, feet planted firmly on the floor, hands resting in your lap. Take full, deep breaths, filling up your lower abdomen with life-giving air and letting your attention sink down out of your head and deep into the rest of you. Let your attention connect to your breath, and let that breath be like a diving bell as you descend deeper and deeper into your body. Taking full, deep breaths, allow your attention to go down to meet whatever feeling, memory, smell, sight, or sound is trying to rise to meet your descending attention. Taking full breaths, you may begin to experience a little lightheadedness—this is normal. Breathing fully, continue to watch whatever arises within you. Staying in your bodily awareness, continue to breathe deeply and fully as you pick up a pen to write what you are experiencing.

Just as I wrote those last ten or twelve words, a big breeze puffed through my window, lifted several pages from my writing table, and flung them to the floor. The earth just exhaled the deep breath I'm asking you to take in and let out. Breathing from the soul-depth, from the depth of the earth, I finish these words.

LOVING THE ARTIST

At a party we are drawn toward someone who "looks artistic," who moves and speaks with wit and confidence, the one with fearless flair. Though we may have come with someone else, we're pulled to this person as if by an invisible magnet. The intensity of our interest draws the person in. Several drinks or lunches or cups of coffee later, we two are an item. Every word of our new beloved seems to fall from those lips like nectar. Oblivious to the Beloved within ourselves, we seek to capture and win an outer Artist.

It is sometimes easier to acquire an artist than it is to access the Artist inside our own body, the one who's been waiting patiently, with fervent prayers for freedom. In the grip of fears we may not even be aware of, we've recoiled from our inventive tendencies, from our natural curiosity, until the small world outside the body seems all there is.

When at last we peek inside and find our Artist, a strong surge of hope passes through us. Rather than attach ourselves to someone else as to a phantom, we can find what we were seeking all along: an unlimited store of truth, beauty, of "all / Ye know on earth, and all ye need to know." We have lain in bed too long staring out the window with longing. When we take the dark leap inside ourselves, we're suddenly awash with ideas, surfing on an endless waterfall of winding turns. Charging into this vastness, we will be left gasping for air if we do not stay close to the felt experience of physical being, to the moment of the breath. Yes, there is urgency. Sometimes the sense of urgency seems unbearable. The tight pressure in the chest, the ache in the heart, the fierce knot in the stomach are real, but they are signals that you've allocated your creativity to some outside source.

By turning inward toward the words we have yet to speak, we own our talent. We claim our life, and the right to write directly from it. We stop entrusting others with that precious part of ourselves. We also have to trust that what we see in others really exists in ourselves. There is an old southern saying that goes, "If you spot it . . . you got it." If we are in a relationship with an artist, we have to learn to trust that we can shine brightly, without dimming their brilliance.

There is brilliance in one who trusts us to spend a good deal of time away, in order to pursue the creative Muse that lives in our cells and tissues, in our bones and blood. A partner can extend love to us by giving us the time we need to be just and true to ourselves.

For all writers, the proof of love of the self as an artist shows in the way we arrange our lives: do we give *ourselves* the time to do what we love, to do what we must?

The Inner Artist is always torn between two worlds: on one side family, friends, leisure, laziness, and on the other the fulfillment of the inner urge to create, to write. How can we honor the Inner Artist? In part, by creating a schedule, a system that is true to the way we write, and true to our physical self.

Do you love to write? Do you love yourself, your true self? Then give yourself time. People often tell me how much they want the grace of their elusive Muse, but they "can't find the time." Or they relate that the people they love need more of their time and that they feel guilty when they go off to write. Find the time. You can't, you won't, write without it. When you carve out time in your schedule to write, then writing truly becomes part of who you are, not just wishful thinking.

I have been lucky, but I have also been intentional. I have looked for and found people who loved me enough to support me in taking the time to write. My partner of over four years knows that I love her, but that that love would be only half what it is if I didn't give myself the gift of solitude every day (and sometimes for a week or two at a time). When I forgo the pull to put pen to paper, when I spend too much time with others, I find myself slipping into artificiality. I don't have as much of myself to share as I do when I'm writing regularly.

To give our best to our writing, we must be willing to give the best to ourselves—to honor our needs, and to stand firm when they are challenged. This is the first courage required of a writer.

SEX AND WRITING

Sometimes what ignites our soul is sex, and sometimes it burns us so beautifully that we stop creating in favor of procreating. We do know that the body is a charge-building system, and one of the few ways our society has taught us to discharge energy is through the sexual act (which is also essentially a creative act). If you have found an artist to inhabit the place in your life where you would be making art, you will make love instead. Except that it will not be *love* you are making. For at the moment of physical union with your outer artist the craving to create art will be amplified. At that moment you will have embodied your yearning. Your body will be aching to give birth, not to a physical child, but to the words of truth that lie dormant within you.

Mary has given birth to three children. The other day at my writing workshop she realized with tears that she had done so out of a repressed desire to create, to write. As she wept, she grieved for what she had not given to her children and for all she had withheld from herself by ignoring her impulse to become a writer. She had decided to bring forth children instead of the songs and poems she is now writing. Mary turned to the group, her face still wet with tears, and said, "What would my children be like if, at the time I brought them into the world, I had been writing from my soul's desire?" Like many other women, Mary had believed that she had to choose between becoming a writer and becoming a mother. As the writer in her withered, her ability to enjoy motherhood also waned.

To achieve balance, to be able to enjoy (and write about) lovemaking in its highest form, you must fall in love with the Inner Artist. Of course, obstacles will arise. Always. One day, sitting across the breakfast table from your Edgar Degas, or your Mary Cassatt, you realize what you have done. When Mary realized what she had done, she vowed to tell her story, so that other women like herself could be helped by her understanding. She had come to realize that motherhood can flourish alongside creative writing. She understood that her creativity had been restored to its natural balance.

Where have you hidden your art? If, reading this, you have caught yourself looking outside for what you already have, turn within now. Use the exercises below to glimpse your inner magnitude. Seeing this truth, you will not fail to write it.

Think of the writers, poets, teachers, and other artists you've been drawn to in your life. Write about how your body ached to do what they were doing. Enter the pain of acquisition and loss. Talk about the pain of continually watching, standing back while others created and you drove the kids to school, went to the office, cooked, watched movies. . . . Now picture yourself as the Artist you are, the Artist you have been all along. Take back all the missing parts of yourself, particularly the creative ones you superimposed over other people. How does that feel? What do you look like as an Artist? How are you going to celebrate this reclamation?

Use your mentality as a writer to create new ways of seeing yourself. Begin seeing your home as the home of a writer, your bed as the bed a writer sleeps in. When people ask you what you do, tell them, "I write," first, then add whatever else you do. When you're tempted to go back to looking outside for clues as to the worth of your words, remember that a writer is simply "one who writes." Remember that the one who writes is you. Remember that if you keep returning to the paper with your pencil ready, you will fall in love with the One inside you who is writing. And that is the beginning of the perfect relationship.

The following exercise will work best if you either have someone read it to you while you do it, or record the instructions onto audiotape so that you can play them back while you do the exercise.

MEDITATION:
MEETING THE INNER ARTIST

Find a private place and time where you can feel
free and uninhibited. Get together your pen or
pencil and paper (or your journal) and place these
writing tools nearby. You may want to put on some
soft instrumental music. Close your eyes. Allow your
awareness to move toward the place in yourself
where the Artist lives. Find the door. Notice what the
door is made of, feel its texture. Is the door ajar, or
closed all the way? Does the door make a sound? Let
the door become alive. Ask the door to show you
the way to the Artist. Follow the instructions you
receive. When the Artist appears, ask questions:
"Where have you been?" "Why?" "How can I help
you get out more?" "What can I do to close the
distance between us?" Invite your Artist to come
with you. If s/he refuses, accept that answer. There
will be other times. Let yourself relax now. . . .
Breathe deeply. . . . Breathe. . . . Breathe. . . . Now
slowly open your eyes. Give yourself a moment to
go over the experience you just had with your Inner
Artist. When you feel ready, begin to write about
what happened.

FEARLESS
WRITING

I believe one has to stop holding back for fear of alienating some imaginary reader or real relative or friend, and come out with personal truth. If we are to understand the human condition, and if we are to accept ourselves in all the complexity, self-doubt, extravagance of feeling, guilt, joy, the slow freeing of the self to its full capacity for action and creation, both as human being and as artist, we have to know all we can about each other, and we have to be willing to go naked.

—May Sarton

WRITING THROUGH PRIMAL FEAR

In my Writing from the Body workshops, both professional and would-be writers have told me that they're afraid of offending others.

Tom has a Ph.D. in physics. He has written a dissertation, has published several scholarly articles, and has cowritten a book in his field. At the age of forty-eight, he is successful by all external criteria and yet he sat with me and cried, saying, "If I wrote how I really feel, it would kill my father and mother. They just couldn't take it."

When you say to yourself, "It would kill them," or "They'd never speak to me again," or "They'd disown me," or "They just wouldn't understand," do you ever wonder, "How is it that I've come to need their approval so desperately that I'm constantly censoring myself?" One answer is that at some time in the past, nearly all of us have felt the terror of knowing that we could not survive without the support of others. Though it may seem only a faint echo in the inner ear, that fear is still with us.

You may not remember it, but probably at around twelve months of age you were in your crib, either hungry, thirsty, or simply aching for attention. You cried out, but just then the telephone rang. Mother, torn between a cry and a ring, answered the phone. Maybe it was a long-distance call, maybe Mother talked into the receiver for what seemed like an eternity. You felt bereft, hopeless. Or perhaps you were out shopping with Dad around age four and somehow his hand, your lifeline in this sea of grown-ups, disappeared. Maybe you wandered around the menswear department of J. C. Penney's crying until you found him. Even if only for a few minutes, you felt the terror that you might never see him again. And how would you survive? "Don't cry, here I am," you were told. So you gulped and swallowed your sobs of relief, exiling them somewhere deep in your bones.

There's no one to blame for these lingering fears. Life is full of separations from the beginning. When these are taken together with other, more obvious and deliberate examples of the cruelties we all encounter in childhood, it becomes clear that nearly all of us everywhere have felt the anxiety of waiting and wishing for a grown-up's return, wondering whether we had been left alone forever.

Maybe you got so used to being left alone that it became a way of life, so that in adolescence you isolated yourself by abusing drugs and alcohol, or simply by hiding who you really were.

When I began to write my first book, *The Flying Boy*, an autobiography in which I revealed painful details of self-abuse through alcohol, as well as the disappointments of my childhood, I knew I risked losing what little connection I had to my parents. During the lengthy process of preparing to write that book, my father and I came as close to each other as men from his generation can get to their sons without the help of a few glasses of bourbon or beer. We endured a strained conversation about my intention to write the book, managing to squeeze in a little affection here and there. Several times my father looked straight into my eyes as I spoke, and at one point he even touched my shoulder.

It was a closeness I'd yearned for as a boy, had given up on as an adolescent, and had denied I needed as a young adult. But finally we were talking. I was telling him everything: how I'd been hurt and how I was trying to heal. He listened, and in his turn pulled loose his part of the story. Together we untangled the years of unspoken misgivings between us. The more we talked, the more I feared losing him as I continued to write my story, making our family's private material public. In spite of my terror, I told my father I intended to write the book. Because of my terror, I begged him not to withdraw from me. Even after my father gave the book his blessing, I still wasn't sure I'd be able to finish it.

Your parents, or other authority figures, may still seem tall and mythic to you. For anyone who was raised to "do it because I said so," parents tend to remain the Alpha and the Omega, the Hera and Zeus who determine our destiny. Coming into your own as a writer involves changing this understanding, letting go of this false image of godlike parents, accepting whatever grief or anger naturally ensues. You must then replace your parents with a higher Self, a worthy mentor. Your parents are the familiar coauthors of your childhood, but you are writing your own story now. To wield your own power, which includes the power of your creativity, you must break free.

Then, instead of skimming the surface of life wearing a plastic mask, you dive toward the teeming colonies—the secrets that lie buried deep in your own consciousness.

Our fear resides in the pit of the stomach, or sits on our shoulders. It tightens the throat and restricts the breath that would lead us toward our greatest subjects, our most exciting and tenderest turns of phrase. When we descend into this fear consciously and consistently for as long as it takes to be done with it, we stop writing half-truths. We begin to tell it *all*. And those ghostly parental or authoritative rhythms that we used to spend so much energy trying to escape, become our allies.

> Before Mrs. Hogendobber had both feet through the front door she had declared that Adam fell from grace over the apple, then man broke the covenant with God, a flood cleansed us by killing everyone but Noah and family, Moses couldn't prevent his flock from worshipping the golden calf, and Jezebel was on every street corner, to say nothing of record covers. These pronouncements were not necessarily in historical order but there was a clear thread woven throughout: We are by nature sinful and unclean. This, naturally, led to Kelly Craycroft's death. Mrs. H. sidestepped revealing exactly how Hebrew history as set down in the Old Testament culminated in the extinction of a paving contractor.

In this passage from Rita Mae Brown's playful mystery *Wish You Were Here*, it is clear that the most familiar rhythms, such as the driving waves of excitement that issue from pulpits all over the South, can propel a writer forward into new territory. Here, the momentum and grandiosity of that rhythm flatten at the end of the section with the diminutive phrase about "the extinction" (not the death, but the *extinction*, as though he were an animal) of a "paving contractor."

You can enjoy the old rhythms. Let them sweep through

your veins, but when the rebellious seven-year-old in you gets the urge to stick out her tongue, let her. That's how the "paving contractor," and the aside about Mrs. Hogendobber's having her scriptural lessons out of sequence, appeared in this piece of writing. It's the writer sticking out her tongue at the preacher. And why not? Who will preserve the wild and childlike impulses of our species, if not the writers? To write well and freely, reconnect with those sudden impulses you had as a child. Attack the sacred cows of your past. It will give you immense satisfaction, not to mention relief, and will carry that satisfaction to others. Your readers want to know that you're no saint, either.

Here's my own example, from a work-in-progress entitled *Long Pants & Sunglasses*:

PEOPLE LIKE THEM

If you grow up in the South trying to be a good Baptist, you're told that you should love everybody. And I've done my best. But despite my efforts, there remains one group of folks that I cannot like.

They can sleep anywhere, anytime, no matter what. They can lie down in the middle of the floor in an airport terminal, head propped on a stuffed animal, backpack or briefcase, and sleep more soundly than I can in my own bed. People may step over them and around them, but they never so much as reveal a twitch of rapid eye movement. They appear to be dead, but they are not. They are happily asleep, and I confess that I hate them for it.

These folks doze soundly on planes no matter how loudly the flight attendant yells into the speaker system. They go to sleep in moving cars as though they hadn't a care, nor the least concern for oncoming traffic. These same snoozers can take two or three naps while watching television at eight-thirty in the evening, then go to bed and conk out as soon as their head hits the pillow.

For some reason, these are often the same disturbed individuals who seldom know the whereabouts of their car keys, and sometimes, their car. They spend an hour each morning before work running from car to house, house to car, searching for the same things they misplaced yesterday.

Worse, these sound sleepers almost always end up living with people like me who can't sleep anywhere but in his own bed—that's on a *good* night. We borderline insomniacs would have to be heavily medicated to be able to sleep in public places. We *could* snooze on a plane, if deprived of three days' rest beforehand. But nothing short of a coma could cause our eyes to remain closed while someone else is driving.

People like me always know where we put our car keys, our sunglasses, and our partners' sunglasses. And though we don't like to admit it, we often know where our neighbors keep *their* car keys.

People like me usually eat about the same time every day, exercise at about the same time, and know exactly what to order in our favorite restaurant—the same thing we had the last time we ate there. People like Them take ten minutes to figure out what they will eat *this* time, and it's usually something they've never had before. They can eat at any time of day or night and, if they go for two weeks without exercising, they don't for a minute worry that Western Civilization will come to a screeching halt.

Do they hate us as much as we hate them? I don't know. Maybe *hate* isn't the right word—"despise," maybe. Yes, that's much better. I don't care what the Baptists say.

It took me almost eight years to realize that I had only told half my truth in *The Flying Boy*. Looking back, I can see that I wrote mostly about my father and very little about my mother's role in my painful childhood. My mother was sacred, as mothers often tend to be regarded. You can say anything at all about Dad, but insulting your mother is undisputed blasphemy. So while I told the truth about my father, I shrouded my mother with silence, until I wrote the final installment of the Flying Boy Trilogy, *Stepping into the Mystery*, which is mostly devoted to demystifying and demythologizing the Mother, explaining how she affects not only our childhood lives but also our adult relationships to women.

I understand now that my connection to my father was so slender and web-like that I never really had him to lose. Very early on I had given up on my father, relying on my mother for love and protection. If my words had "killed her," I thought, then I would surely die soon after. So I waited until midlife, to write my book at a time when I felt absolutely sure that I could take care of myself if my mother "left me."

Where did we get the idea that we have so much power that our words can kill? As a child, you may have bounced, not just on knees, but from opposite ends of an invisible continuum: at one end, you were treated as worthless, just another mouth to feed, and on the other, you were the Chosen One— a saint, a genius, or Savior of the Family. Very few of us received the consistent impression that we were just average, everyday, lovable human beings. So we tend to feel unequal to the high calling of writing. Conversely, we have an image of absolute perfection in the back of the mind: "If I can't write the Great American Novel or at least a *New York Times* best-seller, then what's the point of my writing at all!

Early on, we received notice that our words were all-powerful: "Don't tell your father; it will break his heart," or "These F's on your report card will kill your mother," or "This will just crush her," or "This will destroy him." Are we made of such flimsy stuff? If words could really kill, we wouldn't need bombs or bullets—we would simply approach our enemies, tell them how we really felt, and they'd fall dead in the dirt.

The most destructive words remain unspoken. Waiting for freedom, they stick inside us, undermining our relationships, robbing us of our good health. Have you ever choked back tears in public? Did someone ask, "Are you O.K.?" What was your answer? So often you said, "Fine, just fine," when the real answer, the truer words would have been "Well, as I was driving to work this morning, my heart felt like it was about to explode. In fact, I feel as if an enormous weight were pressing down on my chest, and I think I'm about to cry."

The fear of offending lies deep in our bodies. Marion Woodman says, "As I go deeper, I realize that the voice that says, 'I'm unlovable,' is in the cells. Therefore, it's at the cellular level that the transformation has to take place." We must go to the cells for our truth.

Growing up, we tried to please others. We all did a share of rebellious displeasing, too, but most of us were raised to be "nice," "good," "selfless," without making waves. It's fascinating to watch small children before the truth gets trained out of them. Equally interested in everything, kids call it like they see it, whether it offends or not: "Grandpa, you have a big nose!" or "Why does your chair have wheels?"

Acting "civilized" is another way of adhering to that image of perfection. We're afraid to fail at being nice and polite, although the great men and women we admire are often wild and woolly people who are willing to go out on a limb. What keeps you from following what you admire in others? What keeps you grinning that phony grin? Some part of you still believes your life depends on it.

Body Work:
The Shoulders

Our fear of being left alone can make us feel as if the world were resting on our shoulders. Especially if we feel *responsible* for other adults in our lives, we will tend to carry knots of tension in our shoulders. To give up this tension, try this: Twist a towel into a knot. Feel the tension in your shoulders as it flows out through your arms, out through your hands and into the towel. Repeat this visualization until you feel a release in your shoulders.

As you go back to your writing, feel the difference in your entire upper body, how the loosening flows down through your arms and into your fingers, into the pen or pencil, into the computer keys. Allow this loosening sensation to extend to the words as they shape themselves to the page. Watch the forward flow of language. Become intrigued with its constant, curling reformations. Fall in love with the physical movement of words.

I highly recommend doing this exercise before you fire off an angry letter to a friend or a curt memo to an employee. When you release some of the anger or fear before writing, your words will be more grounded because you will be more grounded in your body. This is also a good exercise for someone who is trying to write a query letter, or a letter of introduction to a prospective employer or college dean of admissions. This exercise can help you reduce the physical tension that prevents your most capable self from appearing in your written words.

MEETING THE SHADOW

Most of us go from relationship to relationship, workplace to workplace, from one social situation to the next, displaying a

pittance of who we really are. We show a *body facade,* and
hide the magical remainder, afraid of what people would think
if they saw our forbidden faces. After all, *we're* afraid of our
dark tendencies. Surely they'd scare other people away! To
write truly and with gumption, you (and I) will have to call a
halt to the Fearfest. Doing so, you'll encounter the greatest
surprise of all, for when the Shadow is carried into the light,
it shrinks to nothing.

At a recent workshop I asked a man to say what had kept
him from writing. This gentleman had been married to the
same woman for fifteen years. He said that if he gave free rein
to his creativity, if he wrote the way he really wanted to write—
indeed, *lived* the way he deeply wanted to *live*—he believed
his wife and children would leave him. He was certain of this,
as if his whole self were a burning bush that might blind both
him and his loved ones. Maybe that's what the burning bush
in the Bible was—a whole Self, the vibrant fire in us that burns
brighter the more truthfully we live. It's possible to become
so used to hiding your burning bushness that the resulting
darkness feels normal. What would happen if you just started
blazing right out in the open?

I asked this man to imagine that his wife and two daughters
were sitting across from him. This is what he told them: "I'm
afraid you'd leave if you really knew who I am. I'm not the man
you think I am, and I'm afraid you wouldn't like me very much."
He discovered that his fear of being left alone was keeping him
from writing the novel he wanted to create. Though you are an
adult, you respond as a child when you feel this fear. The effort
exerted to hide that Child-fear determines the strength of our
Shadow self. The Child's rationale is this: "If my own parents will
leave me if I offend them, then *anyone* will leave. I don't want
to be alone, so I'll pretend." Until you face this fear, the Shadow
will drive the truth out of your life and writing. You can't write
walking on eggshells. Writing from the body cannot take place
in a stiff pose. In fear's tense grip, creativity withers.

You see, as a child you might not have survived had you

been left alone. As an adult, you can't be abandoned by anyone but yourself. If you hold back, you will feel you've been abandoned, and you'll be right—you will have taken leave of your true Self out of fear of the reactions of others.

How can you tell if you've swept your Shadow under the rug when you write? In your novel, look at your characters. Do you love them? Are their idiosyncrasies endearing to you? Or do they bore you? Do you doubt them? Do you feel they are expendable? If your answer to any of the last three questions was "yes," you are probably hiding from your own Shadow. The same is true of details in your poetry or prose. If you write about the pink snow resting on a distant hill at twilight, do you feel and remember that snow? Does it resonate somewhere in your body and breath? You must care deeply about the imagery you include in your work. If you do not find characters in your own work who interest and challenge you, and if you are not deeply affected by the images you've created, then you are hiding from your Shadow when you write.

Just as you are not wholly yourself without your foibles and flaws, so your characters cannot sustain themselves without the muscle that comes from wrestling with demons. See what flaws you avoid revealing in your characters. Notice which situations you edit them out of. The very circumstances, the very "mistakes" from which you rescue your characters, are the very places you must dive into and discover inside yourself.

Though it is often noted that we write to make sense of our lives, it might also be said that we write to pull the rug out from under our feet. We must become so completely grounded that, even as we watch the turmoil of words and phrases and hordes of happenings rising around us, we keep on writing. Writing from the body, we become warriors. In response to an interviewer who asked, "What starts your writing?" William Goyen said, "It starts with trouble. You don't think it starts with peace, do you?" If you are avoiding trouble in writing your story, you are avoiding the really good stuff.

When you pretend too much, in writing and in life, you're

sure to learn that being left alone by others is not the worst that can happen to you. For by your hesitation to uncover the Shadow self, your refusal to become a burning bush, you end up feeling lonelier than ever. You end up feeling that no one really understands you, due to your own conscious decision to prevent them from knowing your depth.

The Shadow is a sleeping giant that every writer must awaken and face head-on, to live and write openly. The Shadow is housed in our bodies and brains, sometimes rising into our awareness through dreams, or through a surprising choice of words we blurt out while chatting. Our prayers and our projections all carry seeds of the Shadow. The people we choose as partners can show us the Shadow in ourselves, as we often project our own undesirable or unwanted qualities onto others.

Our Shadow fears are different depending on the particularities of our upbringing and our belief system. So the material that Marie hides as her Shadow may be the very stuff that Sam glories in telling. But in general we all agree about the nature of the Shadow. It's the dark side: Joseph Conrad's Marlow in *Heart of Darkness*, Poe's Montresor in "The Cask of Amontillado," or Shakespeare's Iago in *Othello*, or Hamlet's uncle. It's the fantasies you harbor that seem so evil you don't want to admit them, secretly fearing, "That must be the *real* me." And it *is* the real you; it's just that it's only *part* of you. It isn't the whole picture.

Here is a poem by Etheridge Knight. I often read it to participants in Writing from the Body workshops, to illustrate the Shadow:

FEELING FUCKED UP

Lord she's gone done left me done packed / up and
 split
and i with no way to make her

come back and everywhere the world is bare
bright bone white crystal sand glistens
dope death dead dying and jiving drove
her away made her take her laughter and her
    smiles
and her softness and her midnight sighs—

Fuck Coltrane and music and clouds drifting in the
    sky
fuck the sea and trees and the sky and birds
and alligators and all the animals that roam the
    earth
fuck marx and mao fuck fidel and nkrumah and
democracy and communism fuck smack and pot
and red ripe tomatoes fuck joesph fuck mary fuck
god jesus and all the disciples fuck fanon nixon
and malcolm fuck the revolution fuck freedom fuck
the whole muthafucking thing
all i want now is my woman back
so my soul can sing

—from *Born of a Woman*

The Shadow reveals itself in any number of ways. But often, as soon as we glimpse it, we recoil and rationalize: we tell ourselves that we didn't really see what we saw in ourselves, or feel what we felt in that moment.

Maybe once you wished for, maybe went so far as to plot, the murder of a parent or sibling. Maybe you had a dream in which you took a machine gun and wiped out all the people at work. Maybe you lusted after a coworker or a friend's spouse. Maybe during lovemaking you suddenly wanted to say and do things that frightened you so much that you were afraid to tell your partner about them. Maybe you've felt jealousy as a colleague made financial gains that surpassed your own.

We dismiss our Shadow feelings and fantasies. We bring ourselves "back to reality." But where do all those feelings go?

Into the body. And there they stay, locked in the stiff back, tight buttocks, hunched shoulders, hardened jaw, sunken eyes. When our bodies freeze up, our pen goes icy, too. What might we write if our body thawed out? No telling, but it would surely be wilder, shot through with inspiration's heat. For the wild writing we're after requires a flaming pen, a pen forged in the fire of the burning bush—the *whole* Self.

Some people let their Shadows run free. Stephen King comes to mind. Here is a writer who lets the Shadow leap onto the page. His books sell millions of copies each year. Why? Something in us is intrigued by the Shadow, despite our fear. Soap operas on daytime television give vent to our Shadow sexuality. And there are the darker examples: pornography is a manifestation of those Shadow selves we have exiled to the netherworlds of our body and psyche. Our society's Shadow jumped out *en masse* when large numbers of people responded to the AIDS epidemic, not with compassion for the dying, but with heightened homophobia—evidence that many of us have disowned certain parts of ourselves.

When we deny the Shadow and try to escape it, when we tell ourselves that it doesn't exist, that's when the Shadow gets nasty. It insists on a life of its own. Its desire is that of every living being: to become manifest in its fullness. If the Shadow is not allowed to show itself honestly and directly, it will manifest in underhanded, inappropriate ways. If I go into a business meeting *ignoring* the fact that I have fear, that I have jealousy and a few greedy tendencies, these characters may leap out and take me by surprise. I may make decisions in that meeting that don't match my true beliefs, my honorable Self.

A more fruitful approach is to humor the Shadow, to enter it and to honor it. It works wonders. I listen to the Shadow's side of things: "Yes, a part of me wants to be sneaky, because if I tell the whole truth to this person I may not make as much money on this deal." There. Said it. I don't have to fear that acknowledging my darker impulses will pull me into the Pit.

I just listen politely with as little judgment as possible and say, "Thank you for your opinion." Then the magic happens: right away I feel new strength to make honorable choices, to go in the way of the Light. Another way is to say a silent invocation, literally to invoke the Shadow ("I can feel myself about to say something selfish and insensitive"), thereby disarming it before it can do any damage.

In our writing, the Shadow often appears as the first paragraph or stanza we write. The ego's arrogance and grandiosity have not subsided yet. But as we write, as we become engrossed in the act of writing, the ego fades, and there is only the steady succession of word upon word, of language creating itself before our eyes. We go back to revise, and there is the not-so-great first paragraph. We cut it out, throw it away. But before we can toss it, *we must let it have its say.* Letting the Shadow speak its piece is part of the process that leads us to the good stuff.

The bottom line: if we're hell-bent on ignoring the Shadow, our writing will not reflect reality. It's not that we all should write Realism. I won't tell you how to write. But if we're to write words that carry the flavor of truth, we have to embrace what is real, in *all* its forms.

If we can't let ourselves go so deeply into the Shadow in ourselves that we fearlessly break all the rules (the way Knight does in "Feeling Fucked Up"), we may never reach the place in ourselves where tenderness resides. The following excerpt from "Belly Song," another poem by Etheridge Knight, completes the picture. We must be willing to feel the darkness, writing past grim obstacles, to get to our truth:

1
And I and I / must admit
that the sea in you
  has sung / to the sea / in me
and I and I / must admit

that the sea in me
  has fallen / in love
  with the sea in you
because you have made something
out of the sea
  that nearly swallowed you

And this poem
This poem
This poem / I give / to you.
This poem is a song / I sing / I / sing / to you
from the bottom
  of the sea
    in my belly

2
This poem
This poem
This poem / is a song / about FEELINGS
about the Bone of feeling
about the Stone of feeling   .
  And the Feather of feeling

3
This poem
This poem
This poem
This poem / is / for ME__for me
and the days / that lay / in the back / of my mind
when the sea / rose up /
  to swallow me
and the streets I walked
  were lonely streets
  were stone / cold streets

This poem
This poem / is /

for me / and the nights
   when I
wrapped my feelings
   in a sheet of ice
and stared
   at the stars
      thru iron bars
      and cried
in the middle of my eyes . . .

This poem
This poem
This poem / is / for me
   and my woman
   and the yesterdays
when she opened
   to me like a flower
but I fell on her
   like a stone
I fell on her like a stone . . .

There's a Babylonian version of the story of Noah's Ark. In this version of the ancient myth of the flood, Noah sends out three birds to bring back a sign that the waters have subsided. First he sends out a dove (the "peace bird"), which doesn't return. Next he sends out a sparrow (a homey image), but that bird doesn't return, either. Finally, Noah sends forth a crow (in the native American religions, the raven and the crow often appear in creation stories). The crow returns to Noah with mud on its feet. A fabulous sign! The waters have receded; it is safe to leave the Ark. Most of us have learned too well how to be sweetly nonthreatening, how to stay aboard the security of our arks. But to feel truly safe and fully free, we have to get mud on our feet.

Where would you go in your body and psyche to find the mud? If you dug in and waded awhile and got really brazen about it, who wouldn't you want to see you that way? Your answers to these questions are the walls separating you from the wild writing you seek to reclaim.

We don't want to write dove poetry and sparrow prose, any more than we want to read it. Writers write to make sense, not of the tidy and the sterile, but of the mysteries, the whispers that have followed us all our lives. We can't stand at the mouth of the cave forever, one foot in sunlight, one in shadow. We have to go into the darkness. Because maybe it's really a tunnel, after all, leading somewhere.

Let your Shadow write a mean poem, or a cruel bit of short prose. Allow the Shadow to spit fire and twirl its mustache. Allow ugly grumblings to creep into the writing. When you've made the piece as mean as you can make it, go one step further—write the unthinkable. Break free. When you're finished, avoid the temptation to judge. Instead, congratulate yourself. You've dissipated the Shadow! Our demons only become dangerous when we shove them into the dark.

Body Work:
The Jaw

Many of us carry in our jaws a number of things we're uncomfortable with—the pettiness of others, or our own. Think about it. When you hear someone, or yourself, make a statement that exposes a wrongheadedness or a "weakness," do you clench your jaw? Often we clench the jaw rather than acknowledge our difficulties, our disapproval of ourselves, our greed, our anger. So fear is also contained in the jaw. To release the emotional energy stored in the jaw, twist a towel tightly and bite down on it. As you do this, let sounds come out of your body. Focus on the jaw, and sound out what is stored there— send it into the towel. You don't need it in your face anymore.

THE DANCE
OF TRUST AND
TIMING

Many of us still have a hard time expressing our lives passionately, dreaming out loud, singing and dancing. Writing, of course, is a powerful Dance, the dance of creation. To write from the body, we must let the body dance. When you're writing well, listening to your body, those rhythms pull the words out to meet them, and all at once you're swinging and swaying in a symbiotic music.

Listen to and feel what happens inside your body when you read this excerpt, the last few paragraphs of a story by Eudora Welty:

"What you doing here, girl?" Mr. MacLain beat his snowy arms up and down. "Go on! Go on off! Go to Guinea!"

She got up and skedaddled.

She pressed through a haw thicket and through the cherry trees. With a tree-high seesawing of boughs a squirrel chase ran ahead of her through the woods—Morgan's Woods, as it used to be called. Fat birds were rocking on their perches. A little quail ran on the woods floor. Down an arch, some old cedar lane up here, Mattie Will could look away into the big West. She could see the drift of it all, the stretched land below the little hills, and the Big Black, clear to MacLain's Courthouse, almost, the Stark place plain and the fields, and their farm, everybody's house above trees, the Maclains'—the white floating peak— and even Blackstone's granny's cabin, where there had been a murder one time. And Morgana all in rays, like a giant sunflower in the dust of Saturday.

But as she ran down through the woods and vines, this side and that, on the way to get Junior home, it stole back into her mind about those two gawky boys, the MacLain twins. They were soft and jumpy! That day, with their brown, bright eyes popping and blinking, and their little aching Adam's apples—they were like young deer, or even remoter creatures . . . kangaroos. . . . For the first time Mattie Will thought they were mysterious and sweet—gamboling now she knew not where.

—from "Sir Rabbit"

Notice how the felt experience of this writing turns and changes within the last paragraph. When a deep shift takes place in your muscles and emotions as you read someone else's work (or your own!), you can be certain you are feeling an approximation of what went through the writer's body at the time of linking those words together. This is the sheer magic of creation, of union. It keeps writers writing.

For the last two days I've been *trying* to write. In other words, I haven't been writing. I've been doing the hundred-yard dash inside my head, worrying about a deadline that's still months away. Yesterday I finally stopped and grew still and listened. I was afraid and sad: scared that my writing is worthless, and sad that I was holed up in a cabin worrying instead of immersing myself in the wonder of the natural beauty that drew me here in the first place.

I stopped writing and walked through the thick multi-layers of green that form the foothills of the Smokies. I wandered down the trails of Desota State Park nearby. I remembered I had come here to wander and explore, as much as to write a book about writing from the body. "Let this body have a little fun!" I thought.

It's strange: when I'm giving a talk, whether to forty or four hundred, I'm loose and free to laugh at myself, even to laugh at the pain we all carry around throughout this cosmic joke called Life. But when I sit down to write, at times anxiety ousts my sense of humor. Instead of sincerity I get seriousness. I get bound up in what I *think* I'm about to say, instead of saying it. William Stafford offers a remedy in his poem entitled "If I Could Be Like Wallace Stevens":

> *The octopus would be my model—*
> *it wants to understand; it prowls*
> *the rocks a hundred ways and holds*
> *its head aloof but not ignoring.*
> *All its fingers value what*
> *they find. "I'd rather know," they say.*
> *"I'd rather slime along than be heroic."*
>
> *My pride would be to find out; I'd*
> *bow to see, play the fool,*

ask, beg, retreat like a wave—
but somewhere deep I'd hold the pearl,
never tell. "Mr. Charley,"
I'd say, "talk some more. Boast again."
And I'd play the banjo and sing.

—from *The Darkness Around Us Is Deep*

I'm learning that "I'd rather slime along than be heroic." Heroes tend to take themselves too seriously. When I'm heroic in this anxious way, my jaw tightens, my brow furrows, my lips purse—and these are just the places I'm aware of. I wonder what happens to the muscles that make up my heart?

Here is a poem by the thirteenth-century Sufi poet and mystic Rumi—gentle but forceful—that says it all, only briefly:

116

Take someone who doesn't keep score,
who's not looking to be richer, or afraid of losing,
who has not the slightest interest even
in his own personality: He's free.

—from *Open Secret: Versions of Rumi*
by John Moyne and Coleman Barks

Later that day I watched horses grazing in the pasture across the little road from my cabin. The sunset was in full glory, and a rabbit nearby began playing hide-and-seek with me. My eyes searched the twin oak trees, so tall that it wasn't certain whether they had been thrown down from the sky or pushed up through the earth.

On this morning's walk I let the satiny breeze carry away my doubts and fears. I could feel that my sadness had settled back into the earth. Then the dance began again, and I had to start writing. I couldn't wait. I didn't want to miss the moment.

I have learned that the body listens to rhythms the mind can't even hear. The wind and the sunset are like a dogwhistle to the bones, but the mind is deaf to their high, clear missive.

Finding your own rhythm for writing is absolutely imperative. What works for Scott Peck, or Amy Tan, or Maya Angelou, or your writing mentor, may not work for you at all. Your body's silent pulses keep time to rhythms playing far down in your soul.

Sometimes I write every day, sometimes no longer than forty-five minutes. On these days, I usually write in the morning because then my body is most alert and energized. Sometimes I get up and write for two hours in the middle of the night, but not often. My body's too fond of sleep.

It used to be that I could only sit down to write for a few minutes at a time. Too soon my loneliness would descend around me. Restless, I couldn't stay with myself any longer than it took to produce short works, brief prose and tiny poems, often only a page or two in length. Then I discovered other writers to turn to, other lonely souls in love with words who wanted to share their work.

We were like new mothers who become a little crazed talking to themselves and to preverbal people all day long in isolation. Suddenly we had each other. With great excitement we shared our new work, shared the miracles and the manias of raising these often difficult children. The support of other writers makes a difference.

As much joy as there is in sharing the work once it has gone beyond the chrysalis stage, we must remain true to the inner call, to the physical push that drives the writing. Once an interviewer asked Eudora Welty, "Do you write for your friends?" Her answer reveals her bold allegiance to the piece of writing itself as it is being created:

> At the time of writing, I don't write for my friends or myself, either; I write for *it*, for the pleasure of *it*. I believe if I stopped to wonder what So-and-so would

think, or what I'd feel like if this were read by a stranger, I would be paralyzed. I care what my friends think, very deeply—and it's only after they've read the finished thing that I really can rest, deep down. But in the writing, I have to just keep going straight through with only the *thing* in mind and what it dictates.

—from *Women Writers at Work: The Paris Review Interviews*

Just as I have become more comfortable writing according to my physical promptings, you, too, will become more who you were meant to be as you continue to write from your body. And just as I felt freer to write when I knew I had good company, you, too, may find your writing time stretching into long and languorous mornings, whole afternoons, and evenings that flash toward midnight. You may write for what seems like only a few minutes, then look up and notice that an hour has passed. Creating this way, we enter a state approaching meditation, where time is fluid and the mind so focused that it folds in on itself and rests, even in the midst of the body's activity.

Timelessness was the unspoken goal of the great artists and architects at the turn of the century. Writers like Thoreau, Melville, London, and Conrad built stories the way John Roebling designed the Brooklyn Bridge, the way Frank Lloyd Wright executed his designs—the work was meant to last forever, to go on luring and fascinating the discerning eye.

For many of us, though, stilling the mind is like trying to seize lightning. Sitting still can be even more difficult. If you find physical stillness challenging, seek out a form of movement that quiets your mental lawnmower. Take long walks. Work in the garden. Practice yoga. As Wallace Stevens said, "Sometimes the truth depends on a walk around the lake." When you return from your mind-cleansing activity, your body will glide into each sentence, your breath inspire each word. For a while, time will become irrelevant, erased.

Recently I was in Colorado leading a workshop, in the ski

town of Snowmass. It's beautiful there, and the people who who live in this community are as gorgeous as their natural surroundings. But during my time there I kept noticing something that bothered me: the condominiums that these wealthy, talented people had built for themselves as getaways. All through the valley stood buildings of dark brown, concrete gray or a deathly blue, in stark contrast to the bright wildflowers, the various greens, the brilliant sky. I realized that what bothered me about these buildings was the same thing that bothered me about some of what I had written in the past: you could live in the writing, enjoy it, be warmed by it, as long as you didn't pay close attention to detail. Like the condos, these writings may be around awhile, but there isn't a lot of detail in them to appreciate on a second or third reading.

Unlike the buildings that went up in the early part of this century, that stood as testaments to the artistry and character of their builders, the condos I saw in Colorado reflected little concern for the creative fire. Contemplating this, I began noticing that my work, though creative in its nature, reflected my hurry to *finish*. Too often I had skipped the refinements of the craft, the carved cornerstone that rewards the discerning eye.

Many of us start our projects with a great burst of energy, but when it's time to dig the gold, when the rush to find the gold mine is over, we tend to race on to the next field, over the next mountain. So the first thing to do is to become aware of this tendency, and the second thing is not to berate yourself about having it. Slow down. Give yourself time to carve that flourish at the top of your building, a reward for the careful observer. Like a newlywed who, long after the novelty of the beloved has faded, lingers to discover what the years will bring, stay with your work. Love it. Joan Didion once told an interviewer,

> I don't have a very clear idea of who the characters are until they start talking. Then I start to love

them. By the time I finish the book, I love them so much that I want to stay with them. I don't want to leave them ever.

Go back to your own writing. Work out the difficult passages. Make sacrifices. Engage. In time, you will know genuine love for your writing. Of course, if it doesn't work out, say goodbye and leave, but softly, without guilt or insult. Don't be afraid to start over. If you remain willing, your soul will build a work that not only satisfies the people of your time, but holds delight a thousand years from now.

AFRAID TO TRUST

I worry that my ink well
may run dry,
that right words
cannot be found.

— Lu Chi

One puts down the first line ... in trust that life and
language are abundant enough to complete it.

—Wendell Berry

Without the ability to trust, it is not only difficult to become a writer, it is impossible to become a healthy, happy human being. Without trust, we become imitators, survivors maybe, but not artists.

As I write this, my left foot is nudging a large stone. Years ago an old lover had the word TRUST engraved on it, and gave it to me for my thirty-seventh birthday. For most of my life I was afraid to trust, not only my creative abilities, but the world at large, and most of the people in it. If, like many of us, you were raised on threats and bribes, trust does not always come easily.

I used to believe my own body had betrayed me. There were times when my insides screamed, "Something's terribly wrong!" and my mother would say, "You're imagining things. Everything's all right." Fear churned in my stomach anyway. My body was telling me that my father was drunk, but what I heard was "He's just not feeling well." I started hating my body for getting so upset over nothing, for telling me "lies."

I can't tell you how many phone calls I've received over the years from skeptical people who called, after having read my first book, to see if I was real.

We have to trust that telling the truth is more important than anything else we can do. We found out as children that telling the truth didn't always bring rewards. We may not yet feel that the truth can set us free. But the freedom is there, if we do as the poet Rilke advised and "Seek the depth of things." If we seek the depth of our personal truth, telling it as boldly and as fairly as we can, we have succeeded.

When you question your personal truth, you stop writing. Lost, you will heed your mental conditioning. Especially if you are writing autobiographically, you may begin to think that, even though you ache to tell things a certain way, you are only exaggerating. You suspect that your memory isn't to be trusted. You forget that it's *your* version to tell. You were there, weren't you? You're qualified. You're only saying, "This was my experience at that moment in time." So much may have changed over time, but our memory of it shows up in the same color, again and again. And that memory is the seed of our truth.

Of course, memory is not real. It's memory. It's not the same as the experience itself. This fact carries an immense freedom in it. It means that everything is fair game—our imaginings as well as the physical events that informed us. Richard Bode expresses this inclusiveness when he writes,

We like to make this artificial distinction between what is fiction and what is fact, what is make-believe and what is true. But I am always surprised when I consider where I met the people who inhabit my memory and who have influenced the course of my life. I met some in the classroom, some in the office, some in the shipyard, and some in the pages of the books I read. David Copperfield and Anna Karenina, Odysseus and Joseph K., Emma Bovary and Sancho Panza are as real to me as my parents, my grandparents, my aunt, my uncle, or any of the characters of my bygone youth who made their livelihood along the Great South Bay.

If we can accept that each of us in the picture—in our family, in our country, in our world—has one truth that is ours and only ours to tell, we can accept the part that is ours to claim and to report. All we have to share is our own perspective of things; if our relatives or our detractors have quibbles, let them write their own version.

What is your truth? Ask your heart, your back, your bones, and your dreams. Listen to that truth with your whole body. Understand that this truth will destroy no one, and that you're too old to be sent to your room.

Move into your truth as though it were an old house. Walk through each room. See, hear, and feel what it is to live there. Try to love what you find, and remember the words that come to you as you explore.

If you embrace it, if you are faithful to it, your truth will reward you with unimaginable freedom and intimacy with yourself and others. You won't land in a world made to order; some people in your life may not like what you write. But those who remain will be allies, people who breathe deeply and listen. It will feel good to be seen completely, and loved as you are. As Natalie Goldberg said after her friend found and read a piece of work-in-progress that she had left out from the day's writing, "I feel good because I don't care that she sees how I really am. I'm glad. I want someone to know me."

When I embraced the truth of my childhood by setting it down in print, it was like finding a whole new family. Hundreds, and ultimately thousands, of people wrote to me saying, "Your telling of your story has allowed me to uncover my own." Many responded by writing their own stories, in their own words. Was telling that truth difficult for me? To say the least. Why did I do it? I simply felt I had no other choice. I had tried every lie I knew, every drug I could find to numb the war that was always being waged inside me—a war between lies and the truth. Finally, there was nowhere else to go. Like someone parachuting out of a burning plane, I dropped out of my head and into the truth. As I dove into my inner darkness, I discovered that I was not inadequate or flawed, only deeply hurt. I was both more and less than my parents had said I was: I was no wormish creature, nor was I a glowing saint. But I did find my own way out.

Now seems a good time to offer you this prose poem written by my friend, Robert Bly:

WARNING TO THE READER

Sometimes farm granaries become especially beautiful when all the oats or wheat are gone, and wind has swept the rough floor clean. Standing inside, we see around us, coming in through the cracks between shrunken wall boards, bands or strips of sunlight. So in a poem about imprisonment, one sees a little light.

But how many birds have died trapped in these granaries? The bird, seeing the bands of light, flutters up the walls and falls back again and again. The way

out is where the rats enter and leave; but the rat's
hole is low to the floor. Writers, be careful then by
showing the sunlight on the walls not to promise the
anxious and panicky blackbirds a way out!

I say to the reader, beware. Readers who love
poems of light may sit hunched in the corner with
nothing in their gizzards for four days, light failing,
the eyes glazed.... They may end as a mound of
feathers and a skull on the open boardwood floor.

—from *What Have I Ever Lost by Dying*

I discovered, as Jean-Paul Sartre did, that "when I began
writing, I began my birth over again," except that this time I
took an active part in the outcome, by wrestling with all the
color and shadow in my body and soul—both the dark and
the light. I trusted that the dark would not kill me, and that
writing about it would not kill anyone else. It didn't. I trusted
that the light would increase as I faced the dark. It did.

I trusted that everything exploding out of my heart and
gut was real, and not just the wild imaginings of someone who
was "too sensitive." I trusted that I could rid my body of its
years of physical and emotional pain, and that in time I would
feel a certain matter-of-factness about these long-lost feelings,
enough that they could become part of a larger story.

Sometimes I feared that I had gone too deep into memory
to find my way back again. But somehow, a semblance of
normalcy always returned. Then I would dive in and write
some more because I knew that, in my case, getting the story
onto the page was healing me, and that I wouldn't be left alone
when it was over.

One sunny afternoon, my friend Bill Stott and I were
walking down University Boulevard in Austin. I was just completing the final draft of *The Flying Boy*. Bill turned to me and
said, "What if no one wants to publish your deeply personal
odyssey?" I looked at him and answered as truthfully as I could,

"Then I'll put it in a drawer and write something else." He looked at me just slightly astonished and said, "You know, I believe you don't really care whether it's published or not." And I said, "You're right. I don't. I didn't write to publish. I wrote so I wouldn't perish, and that's a lot more important to me."

THE BODY'S SILENCE

Tired of all who come with words, words but no
*   language*
I went to the snow-covered island.
The wild does not have words.
The unwritten pages spread themselves out in all
*   directions!*
I come across the marks of roe-deer's hooves in
*   the snow.*
Language but no words.

—Tomas Transtromer
From "March '79"

Try just being still for a few moments. Listen. Music is made not only of sound, but of silence as well. It takes a different sort of listening to hear the harmonics, the blending that takes place in the "silence" between notes, but without it music would be mere disorganized noise. Without measure and pause, there would be no rhythm to our lives, only racket.

Racket, rumblings, and ruminations have stopped my writing for the past two days, in part because I still am not completely comfortable with silence. I feel more at ease when I'm producing something, saying something, making something happen. But so often in silence I find spiritual treasure. As I grow quiet within, a simple humility arises. It is an instinctive yielding to the ways of the natural world, as expressed in the following words by Federico García Lorca:

76

THE SILENCE

Listen, my son: the silence.
It's a rolling silence,
a silence
where valleys and echoes slip,
and it bends foreheads
down toward the ground.

—from "Poem of the Deep Song"

For many of us in childhood, silence meant that something was wrong—the "calm before the storm." Then there was the tense emptiness that followed the storm, when family members passed each other in the hallway without a word. These silences froze our bodies; we watched and waited until the talk began again, a sign that the danger had passed.

Whether or not we dealt with the gale-force words of an angry parent, many of us have the idea that someone's silence is a call to be soothed, satisfied, or sustained. We experience silence as bland, not as the acquired taste it is. We wanted to fill the air with words, to comfort ourselves with a jumble of company.

There are times when I just want to be quiet for a while and let what has been said or done pass through me. Bev, my partner, has this way of settling into herself after we've had a long talk. She needs to be alone for a while, to sift silently through all that we've said and felt together. In the home I grew up in, if you sat quietly, someone was sure to ask, "What's wrong with you?" or "What are you brooding about?"

Childhood is over, though it sometimes seems as if its fears spring eternal. If silence was taboo in your own childhood home, if now you allow yourself to feel how you longed for silence, then you can befriend it.

So many possibilities arise when we respect the body's needs for silence. We become still; we begin to watch. The kind of observation we do as writers often *must* happen in utter silence. It's the same kind of peering we did early on as children: open, without judgment, we see clearly into the souls of people, of animals and objects. Below is an excerpt from Willa Cather's short story "The Old Beauty," which illustrates the clarity of detail that can emerge during the quiet moments:

> Sitting alone that night, recalling all he had heard of Lady Longstreet, Seabury tried to remember her face just as it was in the days when he used to know her; the beautiful contour of the cheeks, the low, straight brow, the lovely line from the chin to the base of the throat. Perhaps it was her eyes he remembered best; no glint in them, no sparkle, no drive. When she was moved by admiration, they did not glow, but became more soft, more grave; a kind of twilight shadow deepened them. That look, with her calm white shoulders, her unconsciousness of her body and whatever clothed it, gave her the air of having come from afar off.

When we embrace our silence, invaluable insights about ourselves and others come to us naturally. It is the simple fruit of moving inward. Not only must we seek the depth of the Shadow in ourselves, but to write from the body we must plumb its silences, where our greatest happiness sits in secret. Because, just as it was in childhood, our quiet contemplation of what goes on inside and all around us is part of the way we play. We have to learn again to give play the dignity it has always deserved: it is the miracle of creation in action, the origin of all true art.

By allowing ourselves to embrace the body's silence, we open the doors to a heaven within. If we go there in earnest, we are not disappointed. Along our search we discover the Voice of the Inner Self speaking through our writing, and the sense of awe we feel is the seed of art.

You may make your way into your writing piecemeal. Begin with a quiet alertness similar to that experienced in meditation. Remain still inside, and the words you are meant to write will come forth. Continue to listen—more words will come. Later, read your own words with an attitude of respect and acceptance. You are uncovering your personal truth. To find this personal truth is no less than finding ourselves, for at the deepest level of being, we are that truth. The drama of our lives carries in it the reflection of the highest knowledge: that we are whole, that we are worthwhile, that we are divine.

Awareness exercise: Find a quiet, private place where you will not be disturbed. Close your eyes and begin to breathe deeply and fully, listening to the sound of your breath. Breathe in . . . Breathe out . . . Breathe in . . . Breathe out. . . . Now take your time as you focus inwardly on the inner feeling of your whole body. Keeping aware of the silence, focus closely on the way your body feels, noting the shape, color, and texture of that feeling. Your awareness will be drawn to a certain part of your body. Focus closely on that part of your body, on the shape, color, and texture of its inner feeling. Stay aware of that part of your body. Ask it, "What do you want me to know?" Be open to whatever answer comes. When you are done, you may want to write about your experience, or you may just want to let the feelings move through you for a while before writing.

Here's a wilder exercise to try: Take a big, overstuffed pillow, or go way out into the country alone, or get into your car and roll up all the windows, and shout as loudly as you can: *"Silence! Silence!"* as many times as you need to, addressing the words to whomever you need silence from. Maybe you needed silence from your parents or siblings years ago. Maybe today you need silence from your husband, wife, boss, or children. When you feel reacquainted with silence, write about it. The time you lived in its still house and walked its soundless hallways. The time you merged with that simple quiet. The time you were most afraid of the lack of sound. Or write a letter to someone you wished for silence from, perhaps someone who wanted to appreciate your ability to keep silence, but who couldn't endure the quiet.

The thirteenth-century Chinese poet Lu Chi says, "Out of nonbeing, being is born. Out of silence, a writer produces a song."

Take all the quiet you need before beginning to write your soul's song. Nourish your body with strong doses of Silence, and do so often. Your silence is as important to your writing as your ability to speak. Even when your body is in motion during the day, listen to the subtle messages inside you. Let these silences reveal their meanings.

Before he lay down for his afternoon nap, the poet Saint-Pol-Roux used to hang upon his front door this message: "The poet is working."

FACING
SUCCESS

*If we are fortunate, we will say something, it will be the
truth, it will be eloquent, and it will have power to it . . . and
we will change our lives.*

—Deena Metzger

While the fear of failure is obvious to many, fear of success, though subtler, is often one of the greatest blocks to writing. Many of us are afraid that success will sever certain of our relationships. Many of those we knew and loved in childhood had such a shattered sense of self that they felt personally diminished when we shone brightly through accomplishments. We may have become hesitant to call attention to ourselves through successes, because we didn't want to risk deepening their dejection.

For as long as Todd could remember, his father had held an entry-level position at work. When Todd excelled in school or in sports he saw that, while his father was proud, there was always a feeling of distance between them. At a Writing from the Body workshop, Todd realized that his father had been jealous of him. Todd's successes had become biting reminders to his father of the way he felt he was failing in his own life. Todd had longed so much for intimacy with his father that he had sabotaged his own success as an adult, so as not to better his father and risk breaking their already tenuous bond.

Robin, too, feared success. Her mother had worked as a journalist at a local newspaper for twenty-five years. Robin's mother lived and breathed the written word, but could never bring herself to risk her secure job with the paper to try writing fiction. Robin knew that her mother had wanted to pursue writing full-time. She also believed that her mother hadn't done so because she had been the sole provider for Robin and her sister.

Robin wanted to write fiction. During the workshop she admitted, in tears, how much she dreaded accomplishing what her mother had not been able to do. Robin believed that if anyone in her family was meant to write fiction, it should be her mother. So Robin had consciously stepped back from the novel she wanted to write. She turned to sales and marketing, and was quite successful in that realm, but she never really felt satisfied.

I've worked with many people over the years who were afraid to "surpass" their parents by fully pursuing their own artistic work, or financial goals. While I taught at a university in the seventies, my own father clung to the fact that he made more money than I. In fact, he gloated. It took me years to understand in how many instances I had shortchanged myself, in attempts to keep him from feeling small. I participated in the myth that my father's worth was measured relative to my own financial stature. If I was making less money than he, he felt wealthy. If I made more, he felt like a poor man. I wanted to preserve his image of himself as the resourceful maverick who had managed to make a good living in spite of a dearth of education and luck.

There is another subtler way that the fear of success shows itself. I have known some writers who resent so fiercely the indignities of childhood that they avoid success to prevent their parents or others from taking credit for their accomplishments. Some writers consciously falter, as if to prove that their parents did a poor job of raising them.

If, as children, we received love and approval only when we made tangible achievements, then as adults we may reason that, if we must be successful to be loved, then to hell with success—and with love!

In adolescence, many of us watched the toll that success took on our peers, the overachievers. In response to such pressure, some young people (perhaps we ourselves) became so single-minded and preoccupied by the drive to perform in academics or sports that little time was left for anything or anyone else. The overachievers were "glowing outcasts," hailed by teachers and parents, but often socially isolated from their peers.

Success *can* carry a price. In my own case, my father no longer speaks to me. A few of my relatives used to think highly of me, but that ended when I told the family secrets and became a fairly successful writer in the process. I have a few ex-friends who rallied around when I was a drunken failure, but who quickly disappeared once I was sober and successful. It threw too much light on their own untried dreams, and their lack of sobriety.

Achieving true success as a writer—that is, successfully expressing your truth—sometimes means risking separation. The key is to surround yourself with supportive people who appreciate your achievements, who can wholeheartedly celebrate your success with you. There are other writers out there who are dealing with the same apprehensions, the same deeply rooted questions.

I found new friends who were not threatened by my victories or diminished by my defeats. Bill, Robert, Caleb, Dan, Marce, Sandy, and others have stood by me while my father grew more and more distant, while my old "friends" decided I had gotten too uppity. Ray Bradbury once said, "Where are your friends? Do they believe in you? Or do they stunt your growth with ridicule and disbelief? If the latter, you haven't friends. Go find some."

If the people you loved as a child couldn't love you as you were, if they envied you or felt intimidated and diminished by your accomplishments, then you must unleash your fear of success before it sabotages your writing and your life.

Write angry letters (don't mail them) to these people and to the "friends" whom you fear alienating. Tell them how you feel about holding back your greatest possibilities so as not to cause them discomfort. Scream into a pillow, *"Don't blame me for being my best!"* Begin the work of finding people who will support and value you, whether you succeed or fail. Share your struggles with them, but share also your splendors—your liveliness, competence, and creative joy.

Writers' support groups exist all over the world. Some are mainly critique sessions, some are warm gatherings of mutual support and encouragement, and the best of them are a generous combination of both. Seek out the writers' groups in your area. If you don't find a good fit, create your own. If you live in an area where you're the only writer, subscribe to the writing journals or magazines that interest you, and consider attending a workshop where you can meet potential pen pals to trade work with. Writing is a solitary practice, but it does not require, nor does it thrive in, complete isolation.

SOME NOTES ABOUT SHARING YOUR WORK-IN-PROGRESS

Once your writing is on the page, it is a separate entity with a life of its own. In a sense, you are its parent. Give it the respect it deserves. Don't allow anyone (especially yourself) to maim it with harsh criticism. Conversely, don't expect it to be as dear to everyone else as it is to you.

If someone else asks to see your writing and you don't want to share it, kindly tell that person that you're not ready for him or her to see it. Though your writings can seem unruly and uncontrollable creatures, you hold the key to the cage. You may keep them locked away for as long as you must.

Frequently the tension we feel due to lack of support—whether physical or emotional, real or imagined—is held in the lower back. When work is done to release this tension, we may encounter memories and impressions that were previously unavailable to us. Such physical "information" can sometimes form the beginning of a story, a poem, or an autobiographical essay. We may remember writing projects we intended to tackle long ago and set aside, or feel renewed enthusiasm for a subject we had forgotten we cared about.

Body Work:
The Lower Back

The lower back is associated with our sense of support. When we feel unsupported by loved ones, or when worry causes us to assume a strained posture, we often experience lower back pain. That pain is actually contraction, tension. This body work will help you release the emotions blocked in your lower back. Before you begin either exercise, sit quietly with closed eyes. Notice the quality of your awareness and the movement of your breath.

1. Stand facing a wall. Bending one knee, lean into a "runner's stretch," palms flat against the wall directly in front of your chest. Go deep inside yourself and imagine the tension flowing up from your lower back, into your arms, and out through your hands into the wall.

2. Position yourself next to your bed, standing well grounded with your feet firmly planted on the floor and knees slightly bent. Using a tennis racket, beat the bed (or couch) with solid, committed strokes. Be careful that you do not arch your back as you come up, as this will strain the back muscles.

Use these lower back exercises to loosen the tension you may have associated with success and its consequences. After completing each exercise, sit quietly for a while, eyes closed. Notice the quality of your physical awareness. Listen to your breath. Is there a difference between what you're experiencing now and what you felt before you started the exercise? Write about this experience.

PUBLICATION AND FEAR OF FAILURE

Do not, for money, turn away from all the stuff you have collected in a lifetime. Do not, for the vanity of intellectual publications, turn away from what you are—the material within you which makes you individual, and therefore indispensible to others.

—Ray Bradbury
Zen in the Art of Writing

One of the fears that most often strangles our desire to write is that we have nothing worthwhile to say. We've been told to "be quiet" so often as children, and this message carries undertones: "You're boring," "You're dumb," or "You're not educated enough to write anything worth reading." We carry these pronouncements in our bodies like dormant illnesses.

We all have something important to say. The position I

take in writing workshops, and here in this book, is that we all
have at least one book inside us. But we find it hard to believe
Ray Bradbury when he says that "every man will speak his
dream. And when a man speaks from his heart in his moment
of Truth, he speaks poetry." To accept that we're *all* poets and
writers seems a bit extreme. But pure poetry is produced all
the time, leaping out when we least expect it. I recently spoke
with a farmer who said that he'd seen "two squirrels on a wire
that ran so fast I thought I saw gray smoke on the telephone
line." Metaphor in action. And, as Bradbury goes on to say,

> I have heard mothers tell of the long night with their
> first born when they were afraid that they and their
> baby would die. And I have heard a grandmother
> speak of her first ball when she was seventeen. And
> they were all, when their souls grew warm, poets.

If we turn to our deepest longings, our most heavily
guarded secrets, to the wild strains that play in our blood, then
we will have volumes to say. But if we are to speak freely, we
must first recognize the malignant messages we carry, and rid
the body of these toxins. We must discharge the pent-up emotion that pen and paper may not be able to reach.

If we can trust this process, delving far enough to find
what is truly ours, we will experience the power in our words,
just as we can reclaim the energy that is stored in our bodies
as tension: the original power behind our anger, grief, and fear.
Because the power of the Word is indestructible, unchanging,
eternal. It carries within it the first breath of life. And whether
it resides in our bodies as stress, or in our written work as
language capable of uplifting humanity—still it is *there*. Once
we realize the immensity of the treasure still untapped within
us, we begin to see our negative beliefs about ourselves as
opportunities. How can we resist the challenge of transforming
a misshapen myth into a crystal truth? How can we resist the
challenge to return to joy?

Many of us were taught as children that our perception of reality was flawed, inferior, or just plain inaccurate, so we began to look to others to translate reality for us, to recommend activities worthy of our time and energy. We learned that other people, bigger people, were powerful. Slowly and silently, we disowned our precious birthright of independent thought and action.

We watched the "power figures" in our lives to find out how we were doing. And all the while *they* were measuring *their* progress based on *our* successes and failures, and on the reactions of others in *their* lives. A vicious cycle, without winners. We began to see through twisted glasses in which every endeavor became a kind of groping, a desperate means rather than a joyful end. We became the means to others' happiness; we were charged with propping up their sense of self. As long as we lived so as not to ruffle anyone else's tenuous sense of well-being, we "succeeded." We got the love, affection, and attention we needed—as long as we didn't make anybody mad.

As writers, many of us still unconsciously seek approval from the publishers and readers of this world. When we receive their criticisms or their accolades, it isn't only our written work that is being appraised. We are listening for signs of our human worth. Such outward seeking stifles our creative work, because as we guide our writing through its fragile state of becoming we cannot afford to look backward, or side to side. We must stay fixed on the course ahead, surely and steadily traveling forward. If we try to write for an editor or publisher, we bind our own feet. By forcing our writings into a smallness that can never contain their possibilities, we ultimately cripple them.

There is nothing small about creativity. It is no less than the most powerful force of nature. All creative acts, like the act of making love, should be strong in beauty, and in rhythm. Our writing can be ecstatic, wild, and strange, but it must be *real*. We can't reach the state of creation, the state of truth in our words as long as we're busy thinking: will they like it? I doubt that Pulitzer prize-winner Paul Zindel spent much time wondering whether people would like his play, as he wrote this monologue for Tillie, the young student who discovers the wonders of science through her high school project in *The Effect of Gamma Rays on Man-in-the-Moon Marigolds:*

TILLIE'S VOICE: He told me to look at my hand, for a part of it came from a star that exploded too long ago to imagine. This part of me was formed from a tongue of fire that screamed through the heavens until there was our sun. And this part of me—this tiny part of me was on the sun when it itself exploded and whirled in a great storm until the planets came to be.

[*Lights start in.*]

And this small part of me was then a whisper of the earth. When there was life, perhaps this part of me got lost in a fern that was crushed and covered until it was coal. And then it was a diamond millions of years later—it must have been a diamond as beautiful as the star from which it had first come.

TILLIE [*Taking over from recorded voice*]: Or perhaps this part of me became lost in a terrible beast, or became part of a huge bird that flew above the primeval swamps.

And he said this thing was so small—this part of me was so small it couldn't be seen—but it was there from the beginning of the world.

And he called this bit of me an atom. And when he wrote that word, I fell in love with it.
Atom.
Atom.
What a beautiful word.

Tillie's wistful repetition of the word "atom" gives us the pleasure of a double understanding. We remember the biblical creation story of Adam, the first man, and Eve, the first woman. Such surprises may or may not be planned by the writer at the time the pen touches the paper, but in any case, they seldom occur while we are worrying about what to say next. More often we become caught up in the imagery and the rhythm of the moment. We are adrift on a vision, riding the feel of language, the excitement of getting it all said.

Yes, it is possible to write to please others and get published, but why would anyone want to? As Bonnie Friedman says in *Writing Past Dark*, "If you give away part of yourself, then you feel lean and hungry, you long for what you've given away. If praise comes it satisfies only briefly. How could it be otherwise?"

We all know too well "you can't please all the people all of the time," and yet some of us go on trying. Our writing will usually fail to excite some of the people, most of the time. Our writing should take us far enough inside ourselves that we discover our truth, and glory in that discovery without ever "thinking" about it. Practiced for sheer joy, as an end in itself, our creative work can satisfy a part of our souls that no publisher can ever fulfill.

When we learn to treat ourselves as lovable, when we humor our failings rather than turn up the volume on our self-criticism, we naturally begin to regard our writing with the same love and good humor. To do this, we take action to free up the long-stored tensions that block our bodies and our potential for contentment. In the process, we lower the volume on the negative messages.

Your mind is innocent: it feeds back whatever has been put into it. As a writer, you must teach your mind the truth that success as it is measured in the world does not matter an inch. It may line the pocket, but it will never cause the heart to soar. You must teach this lesson to your mind again and again, because it is forgetful and fond of its habit of nagging you to "do better."

What does writing for writing's sake feel like? An ache, an urge in the body that can only be soothed by descending into the deep center of yourself and snapping up words like silver fish. If you enter the writing in a worried and fearful state, you will poison the water, and your words will float to the surface belly up.

As a graduate student, I was heavily invested in being seen as smart, well-read, definitely "doctoral material." With this outward focus, I couldn't follow the advice given by Brenda Ueland in her wise book *If You Want to Write*:

> You must feel when you write. . . . You must disentangle all thoughts. You must disconnect all shackles, weights, obligations, all duties. You can write as badly as you want to. You can write anything you want to . . . just so you write it with honesty and gusto and do not try to make somebody believe that you are smarter than you are.

I had been using all the talents at my command to impress other people. I wanted my father to see me as a mental Superman; I wanted my professors to see me as "an intellectual." I was an impostor. I felt angry and resentful toward the professors I was trying to dupe, as though they were somehow to blame for my insecurity. Eventually, though, I had to let go and simply write. I found that the act of writing itself sustained me, and I gradually set aside the desire to publish.

I have read so many words written to prove something to someone. Such prose or poetry doesn't touch me because it has a predatory motive: it's unconsciously tracking down an audience. I don't trust such writing because it attacks me. I feel devoured rather than addressed. I couldn't recognize this kind of writing if I hadn't practiced it myself.

Writing that pops out of the head full-blown, dragging all its reasons and agendas behind it, drains my energy. But writing that issues from the body *bestows* energy. It grants an intensity to both writer and reader. William Blake said that "energy is eternal delight."

Write for yourself—always. So often the instructions we receive in so-called writing courses is of little benefit. We've been told, "Know your audience." I remember once sitting for hours, pen frozen in hand, wondering who I was addressing. Worry stops our work.

You don't need to know very much about your audience, but you do need to know yourself—deeply, fearlessly. When you come to know your true Self, you will naturally come to know others. You reach the fountain within you that sustains you, and sustains your writing. You will begin to find in your life and work the meaning you crave. Then delight will come to you as easily as a tear to a tender soul. As Robert Bly says, "The world scorns football players who make no yardage, writers who do not publish. . . . But the Soul truth . . . sustains us and we receive nourishment from this truth." When we can live from that Soul truth our lives will also benefit the lives of others. Our practice is to put our faith in the art of truth, and not in artifice.

We must labor to remember our first reasons for wanting to create. As children we stirred up mudpies, spent hours raising sandcastles, building huts from fallen branches; why? Because to create is a natural response to joy. It is simply what we human beings do. We didn't begin creating for any outward result. We did it for the fun of making something that wasn't there before. The work of every true writer is to remove everything that stands between oneself and one's original state of joy.

In his book *Once Upon a Midlife*, Alan Chinen tells an Indian tale in which a master craftsman extracts gold and silver from a forest in order to fashion "wondrous objects." But the craftsman never tries to sell his work. Instead he melts down his creations and makes new ones. In the tale, the Queen becomes puzzled by this peculiar way of working and asks the

reason for it. The old man explains, "It's the creating I enjoy."
It's what we did *first*. We can do it again.

Here's a chance to write about what it was like to
feel that you were a means to someone else's
unknown ends—what it was to let yourself be stifled
by someone else's expectations, whether parent,
partner, lover, or boss. Write what it was like to feel
like a producer instead of a person. Write about the
longing to be loved, accepted, embraced for who
you are, not for what you accomplish. Afterward, you
may want to write about a time when you, in turn,
imposed your own expectations on someone else.
Remember again as you write that the goal is to
enjoy your Self, not to impress.

Take a minute to go inside yourself to the part of
you that's caged off and blackened by negative talk.
Listen to those familiar "you can't do it's" for a
minute, then let the feelings come up and out of
your mouth with sighs, groans, or yells. Or let them
come out of your eyes as tears. If you feel really
angry about what you heard, then take a towel and
twist it as hard as you can, letting out any sounds
that may be buried deep in your back. Don't hold
back.

TAMING THE
CRITIC OR
LIGHTEN UP!

*If you're not afraid of the voices inside you, you will not
fear the critics outside you.*

—Natalie Goldberg

When we begin to take seriously the ways in which we have
stored unresolved experiences in our bodies, when we begin
in earnest to learn to release these emotions and to give them
their physical say, our writing is ignited. We begin to take our
lives seriously, and thus we begin to face death: it is the cold
fact that shakes us awake to the depth and value of life. By
keeping the fact of our mortality in view, with greater humility
we seek to master the creative power of breath. We accept air
into our lungs as a gift. We begin to write with a new conviction—with *duende*.

What will we do with this wisdom? Will we run from the

truth all our lives? Or use it to sing? In *The Writing Life*, Annie
Dillard writes,

> Why do you never find anything written about that
> idiosyncratic thought you advert to, about your fasci-
> nation with something no one else understands? Be-
> cause it is up to you. There is something you find
> interesting, for a reason hard to explain. It is hard to
> explain because you have never read it on any page;
> there you begin. You were made and set here to give
> voice to this, your own astonishment. . . .
>
> Write as if you were dying. At the same time,
> assume you write for an audience consisting solely
> of terminal patients. That is, after all, the case. What
> would you begin writing if you knew you would die
> soon? What could you say to a dying person that
> would not enrage by its triviality?

What happens when we don't take our pain, our pleasures,
and our mortality seriously? If we can't honor and embrace
the disappointments as well as the "successes" in our lives?
We overcompensate. We take our writing, our "artist persona,"
much too seriously. We fall out of balance.

These are the origins of the suicidal starving-artist syn-
drome, the one whose life folds in on itself and gets trapped
in the Box of Perpetual Gray. Rather than understand and write
from the dark, sweet center of Life, our attention becomes
focused on the agony of artistry. All the while, the most important thing going on is that the unfinished business—disguised as our tense shoulders and tight neck—is vying for our
attention.

Once we take seriously our bodies, our pain, our health,
we're free to lighten up. We relax not only our demeanor, but
the demands we've placed on ourselves to create Serious Art,
as if our lives depended on that.

The world doesn't really *need* another book. Have you

been to a bookstore recently? A public library? It's staggering, isn't it? We don't *need* to add another star to the night sky. But it is gratifying to make art from our experience. William Goyen says, "Writing is an act of hope and faith. Art is redeeming, and an act of affirmation. *There's no other way.*"

What we do need is writers—people—willing to get intimate with the truth that lives inside them. The various murders that take place every day, whether murders of the body or of the tender spirit, are committed by those who have turned away from the simple truths inside themselves. *This* is serious business. Yes, we can inform, create change, and elevate the human experience through writing. But such writing is only born of a life actively engaged in the thick of things. First we have to stop torturing ourselves, stop locking up our feelings in the Black Box. Engaged in this more personal struggle, we can become instrumental in effecting the changes we seek in the world.

In other words, once we're fully engaged in and committed to the process of our own healing, we will have something valuable to say. Still, we do so from a place that's less serious than it was when we were only interested in getting our books into print. If we devote body, soul, and brain to the cause of righting our inner imbalance, to freeing the emotions locked in our bodies, eventually we will begin to feel fine, *whether we write or not*. We will discover how our writing fits into the bigger picture. We begin to notice when we're not having fun with our writing—we recognize it as a sign that our truth has slipped into the background. That truth may consist of hidden grief and hurt, or our natural sense of fun and joy that's been shoved underground.

We know we've lightened up our expectations of what our books will do for humanity (or perhaps more accurately, for our self-esteem) when we don't consider our writing more or less serious than the challenges of gardening, cooking a good meal, or working on the car. When we engage in our lives with full breath, body, and soul, then every act carries in it an echo of the sacred. Holding a sleeping child, melting butter in the skillet, spending the morning writing—all have equal capacity to bring great satisfaction.

As we begin to attain this outlook on our creative output, we understand William Blake's attitude when he said, "I will not reason and compare. . . . my business is to create." We recognize the creative essence inherent in all our activity, and we get on with it. In our writing, this attitude keeps our attention focused on what needs to be said, and the words needed to say it. If the critics out there want a listening ear, they can find it elsewhere.

By the time you read this, a beautiful little book called *The Bridges of Madison County* by Robert James Waller will have sold five million copies and the movie probably will have been made. The book has already sold three million copies at the time of this writing. *Bridges* is the only novel I've ever read in one sitting. It made me cry right out loud on the plane I was taking from San Francisco to Juneau. Yet most of the literary critics hated it. But when a written work fuels our lives, when it calls to something so deep in us that it makes us abandon our usual "stiff upper lip," then I stand behind it.

I want to be honest with you. I still sometimes long for validation from outside myself. I still ask others, "How am I doing?" I want to be clear that I'm not yet able to write solely from the body. If I didn't need to learn this material myself, I'm sure Life wouldn't have charged me with teaching it. I still pay a little attention to "critical" success. But I'm working on it. Each year I seem to take my critics and myself a little less seriously. And perhaps this is just the way it is—the more seriously you take your "art" or "ideas," the more seriously you take the critics' assessment of them.

Still, the critic we usually fear most is the one who lives inside us: the voice that tirelessly repeats those derogatory remarks I spoke of earlier. Sometimes it seems this voice never sleeps. Imagine the kind of work we will write when our ears become deaf to its objections!

This belittling inner critic lives in the body, and has been there since early childhood. This Negative Critic has nothing to do with your writing. It has to do with your being who you truly are. The Negative Critic knows little, but has all the confidence of a prizefighter. It's the gnarly ego, strutting and whining, finding fault everywhere. It often sounds like someone in your immediate family: father, mother, sibling, uncle, grandparent, or teacher. To call this critic out of the brain and body, you must assume a warrior's stance. You must meet the Negative Critic the way you meet your own Shadow—head-on. By challenging its lies, you give life to the gentle critic within you, the trustworthy and helpful guide who guards the clarity of your truth.

This True Critic is firm, but kind. It often appears after I've written the first burst of a piece I'm working on. I let this voice have eyes and ears as it goes over the first, rough draft. The True Critic is honest, and seeks out what isn't working. The message of the True Critic is "Let this writing have its own life. Cut out the frills, and write toward the simple truth."

On my good writing days, I don't let the Negative Critic appear until I'm finished with the first draft. On my great writing days, I don't let the Mean Critic (who sounds a lot like my dad: "You're too dumb to write!") appear at all.

On those good days, I don't take my writing or my books too seriously. I dance with the words and let the feelings in the words take the lead. I play with phrasing and imagery like a child fashioning a city with blocks. If the whole thing collapses, I start over. On good days, I know and feel that the world will hold on to its place in the heavens whether or not I write another word. I move through the pages like a whirling dervish, winding among language that flows from its own wild center. And in my spinning, both kind and unkind voices fall away. I spin to see God, to feel the thrill of God, and nothing else.

The following poem by Rumi quickly returns us to center. It illuminates both the body's wisdom and its failings, as well as the attitude we must take toward the body if we are to find and speak our truth:

> *On Resurrection Day your body testifies against you.*
> *Your hand says, "I stole money."*
> *Your lips, "I said meanness."*
> *Your feet, "I went where I shouldn't."*
> *Your genitals, "Me too."*
>
> *They will make your praying sound hypocritical.*
> *Let the body's doings speak openly now,*
> *Without your saying a word,*
> *as a student walking behind a teacher*
> *says, "This one knows more clearly*
> *than I the way."*

—from *This Longing*
  translated by Coleman Barks

WILD WRITING:
RESISTING THE
URGE TO CONTROL
AND CONFORM

. . . in literature it is only the wild that attracts us.

—Thoreau

Have a lot of nerve. Fall down big, make a big splash.
Why not?

—Marvin Bell

. . . I know I live half alive in the world. Half my life belongs
to the wild darkness.

—Galway Kinnell

In her wonderful book *Living by Fiction*, Annie Dillard says, "The span of fiction's movement in this century has been narrower than that of painting, but the direction is the same: from depth to surface . . . from story to theory . . . from emotion to mind." The wild is mostly gone—the premeditated is everywhere. We sit and think, and then we sit and write. Dillard goes on to say that "at some point the people in novels stopped galloping all over the countryside and started brooding from chairs. Everything became psychological and interiorized. External conflict became internal tension." The wild that Thoreau longed for and went seeking during his days at Walden seems nearly gone for good. The wild days—like the day Thoreau saw a squirrel dart in front of him and he had the urge to grab it and devour it alive—are nonexistent for civilized folk.

Little of what we read has this raw quality. We've distilled everything down in the brain's pressure cooker. At rock concerts, listeners sit stolid, occasionally swinging a foot or patting a leg. We clap only if someone else does. If one of us does have the courage to rise and dance, everyone turns to get a look at the "drunkard." Are the dancers really the ones out of step? The body is *dying* to express its truth in movement. This is why so many pink people dream of a Sunday in a black gospel church, where we could feel free to sway and swoon in the Spirit.

For too long we've been shut in the tiny apartment of our minds, keeping a neatly ordered structure, labeling things "good" or "bad." You can observe this in your own writing. Every once in a while a stray thought, a wild notion, tromps in on its muddy boots. And do we shoo it away? No, we love it. Even if we feel a little guilty for loving it, even if it spots the pristine floor of our preconceived notions, we find ourselves charmed and moved by wildness. Here's further evidence: Clarissa Pinkola Estes' best-selling book, *Women Who Run with the Wolves*, explores the wild in the soul and psyche of Woman. Robert Bly's book about Iron John, the Wildman in the woods, a huge success, became a bible for the growing men's movement. And while dead writing is still taught at some universities, young writers in search of the Wild look to Walt Whitman, to the establishment-bashing poets of the sixties, to the wild surrealists writing in war-torn countries where poetry—especially overtly political poetry—is risky business.

Some of us, recognizing the need for wildness, have imitated the personal habits of the wild writers, rather than their brilliant creative impulses. So many writers have turned to alcohol and drugs to let go of enough inhibition to enter the uncharted with daring. But such artificial methods eventually wear thin, taxing the body so severely that its words grow cynical, passionless. Writers like Edgar Allan Poe fuel our imaginations, yes, but at what cost to themselves? We can't borrow our wildness from substances, or from other people's lives. And we don't *need* to borrow it! We have our own wild nature, though it may still lie dormant inside us, aching to be freed.

THE JAR WITH THE DRY RIM

The mind is an ocean ... and so many worlds
are rolling there, mysterious, dimly seen!
And our bodies? Our body is a cup, floating
on the ocean; soon it will fill, and sink ...
Not even one bubble will show where it went down.

The spirit is so near that you can't see it!
But reach for it ... don't be a jar
full of water, whose rim is always dry.
Don't be the rider who gallops all night
and never sees the horse that is beneath him.

—from *When Grapes Turn to Wine: Versions of Rumi* by Robert Bly

True passion, true wildness is never dry. It can *contain* dryness, even hatred or cynicism, but it springs from a deep love of living, a fascination with life's intricacies, its unpredictable appropriations of persons, places, and times. The true wildness is natural, yet surprising. By entering what is untamed in us, we break through the barriers of years of habits, we break through tired concepts and tendencies that would drive our strangeness underground. To experience our wild writing, we must seek the depth of ourselves. We must go far and fast, with little thought of how we will get out of this mess. And, unlike those who have sought wildness through addiction or obsession, we must live to tell the tale.

Since early childhood, we have been trained to stay in control of ourselves, our fantasies, and most certainly our bodies. Somehow we learned to shut down our spontaneous responses to life—our moods, our quirky ideas, the flood of emotions called up by the most memorable events of our lives. We hid ourselves by keeping a controlled exterior. We desperately hoped that, through twenty-four-hour-a-day hard work, we'd be able to pin down the people, places, and things in our world, force them to line up single file. Of course, this futile endeavor exhausted us. At times we may have thrown up our hands and cried to the heavens, wondering if some sense of order was too much to ask.

Control douses the fire of our wildness. To touch what is truly wild, to give ourselves over to the throes of invention, we set set sail into strange waters. While we are writing, we have to be free enough to run naked, to hop on the backs of giant wolves and ride into the deep woods without looking back.

Below is a piece of short fiction. As you read it, notice the sense of discovery inherent in the fabric of the writing, how what happens seems to flow inevitably from the storyteller's voice. Hear the wild and earthy music of that voice, how it paints the scene in all its physicality:

BLIND GIRLS

She knew it was only boys in the field, come to watch them drunk on first wine. A radio in the little shack poured out promises of black love and lips. Jesse watched Sally paint her hair with grenadine, dotting the sticky syrup on her arms. The party was in a shack down the hill from her house, beside a field of tall grass where black snakes lay like flat belts. The Ripple bottles were empty and Jesse told pornographic stories about various adults while everyone laughed; about Miss Hicks the home-ec teacher whose hands were dimpled and moist and always touching them. It got darker and the stories got scarier. Finally she told her favorite, the one about the girl and her boyfriend parked on a country road. On a night like this with the wind blowing and then rain, the whole sky sobbing potato juice. Please let's leave, pleads girlie, It sounds like something scratching at the car. For God's sake, grumbles boyfriend, and takes off squealing. At home they find the hook of a crazed amputee caught in the door. Jesse described his yellow face, putrid, and his blotchy stump. She described him panting in the grass, crying and looking for something. She could feel him smelling of raw vegetables, a rejected bleeding cowboy with wheat hair, and she was unfocused. Moaning in the dark and falsetto voices. Don't don't please don't. Nervous laughter. Sally looked out of the window of the shack. The grass is moving, she said, Something's crawling in it. No, it's nothing. Yes, there's something coming, and her voice went up at the end. It's just boys trying to scare us. But Sally whined and flailed her arms. On her knees she hugged Jesse's legs and mumbled into her thighs. It's all right, I'll take you up to the house. Sally was stiff, her nails digging the skin. She wouldn't move. Jesse tied a scarf around her eyes and led her like a horse through fire up the hill to the house, one poison light soft in a window. Boys ran out of the field squawling.

—Jayne Anne Phillips
from *Black Tickets*

There is a certain amount of recklessness involved here, a certain "I don't care what anybody else thinks," a sideways-ness, a bizarreness. "If you feel like a murderer for the time being, write like one," says Natalie Goldberg. Wild writing comes when you've forgotten to try to please anyone else, when you've forgotten about publishing. It comes while you're pretending there's no tomorrow, when you're writing head-on, full of breath and vigor, words trailing behind you in a fiery blaze. You keep riding, riding, riding that trail of words, holding for dear life to the reins, ignoring the dust in your teeth and hair. You ride to get to wherever you're going, and nothing stops you until the trail wanes to a dead end of faltering phrases. Then you rest, satisfied. You turn and marvel at the lines of text stretching off into the distance.

There's nothing wrong with self-control. We all recognize that children need to learn it early on. Our self-control gets us through tense conflicts without screaming or hitting. It keeps us from spending money wantonly, from eating past the healthy point. It keeps us from doing things we'd regret. Self-control has its place. But that place is not in the midst of the creative process. While we engage our hands, our breath, our minds at the moment of writing, we must be free. Self-control comes later. It's part of the process of revision.

The energy that creates the wild writing is the same energy that fuels the dancing, shouting, and singing in a soulful gospel church. It's the same energy that pulls the listener from his seat at the rock concert and makes him a dancer. That wild energy exists in making love without an agenda or a clock. It makes possible the two-hour bath. It's holding your baby in your arms as she nurses, never minding the pull or the length of time she needs to take her nourishment. It's letting go completely, embracing what happens.

Watch how the following short fiction by Joyce Carol Oates makes us stop everything, hanging on each new detail she offers:

SLOW

The wrong time for him to be returning home so she stands at an upstairs window watching as he drives up the driveway but continues a little beyond the area where they usually park in front of the garage and stops at the car back by the scrubby evergreen hedge and then there's another wrong thing, it's that she doesn't hear the car door slam, she listens but she doesn't hear, so she turns slow and wondering from the window goes downstairs and at the door where there's still time for her to be hearing his footsteps she doesn't hear them so like a sleepwalker she continues outside moving slowly as if pushing through an element dense and resistant but transparent like water and at the end of the walk she sees that he is still in the car still behind the wheel though the motor has been turned off and the next wrong thing of course is that he's leaning forward with his arms around the wheel and his head on his arms, his shoulders are shaking and she sees that he is crying . . . he is in fact sobbing . . . and in that instant she knows that their life will be split in two though she doesn't, as she makes her slow way to him, know how, or why.

—from *The Assignation*

It is a wildly attentive voice that reports the vision of the man and woman. We listen as if peering over the shoulder of the woman watching the scene. Oates' allegiance in the writing to that feeling of waiting and wondering, of alternate fear and hope, conveys the moment with a physical immediacy. We merge with the woman, wait with her, holding our breath, full of imaginings about what will happen next. It is only through releasing ourselves completely from the rules and rattlings of the mind that such writing is possible.

There's an exercise I sometimes use in workshops: Make the ugliest face you can possibly make. Some people can make horrid faces, and others can't release control even for the minute or two required, even though I'm setting my own gruesome example right there with them.

Some people have driven their bodies on automatic for years. They make love the same way every time. They don't make a sound when they cry. These are the same people who, when they sneeze, cover their face and hold it in, nearly blowing their brains out with the implosion. These are the people who want to be held, but who ask, "Would *you* like a hug?"

When we're stuck and controlled like this, our wildness is stuffed down in some lonely corner of the body—the back, the buttocks, the shoulders. We take a few drinks of scotch and the wildness rolls and roars forth, but this is not authentic wildness. It has a savage quality, and can turn brutal. True wildness is wonderfully free. It contains an element of grace, of ultimate goodness. It hurts no one. By releasing itself into the open air, the energy of wildness does what comes naturally: it begins to create, and wild writing is born.

Try completely letting go of control and writing wildly for ten minutes. Just move your pen across the paper in whatever way your wild hand wants to move—like a mother wolf playfully pawing her cubs, like a deer punctuating the forest on fast hooves. Make sounds as you write. Write from the spirit of any animal whose image pops into your body/mind. Write without thought or worry. Write out all the tensions and the tightnesses you've been carrying. Write with nothing in mind. Write empty and wild, and then ask yourself the question Ray Bradbury asks: "When was the last time you dared to release a cherished prejudice so it slammed the page like a lightning bolt?" What are the best and

the worst things in your life, and when are you
going to get around to whispering or shouting
them? Wildly? Passionately? Positively, without a trace
of doubt? Let go and write from your whole Wild
Body.

Writing in color: Mixing up the senses (synesthesia)
is a great way to break old habits of seeing and
feeling. Tomas Transtromer once wrote, "Feel the
smell of truth."

*This exercise will work best if read to you by
someone else, or if you record the instructions on
audiotape and play them back as you follow along.*
Choose one of the words below. Speak it
distinctly, feeling the word on your tongue and
teeth, feeling its vibration in your larynx. Close your
eyes and say the word again. What color is it? If you
don't "see" a color, what color do you *feel* when
you say this word? Do this with any of the words
that interest you, then come up with some of your
own words to experience in color. Use this
experience to begin a writing session, to shake you
out of your usual ways of thinking.

hobgoblin	*style*	*flinch*	*guarantee*
carpool	*artichoke*	*smackeroo*	*whisper*
abrasion	*rubber*	*sniffle*	*toot*

Body Work:
The Abdomen

We tend to store a "band of fear" throughout the abdominal region. When we loosen the abdomen through body work, we're able to breathe more deeply, to feel life-giving air coursing through our bodies, and to write from that place of fullness.

1. Much of body work is transferring the tightness in our bodies into some physical form outside ourselves. To rid yourself of "knots in the stomach," take a towel and twist it very tightly, so tightly that it begins to curl upon itself, forming a knot. Be conscious of your abdomen as you do this. Breathe deeply, and exhale any sounds that naturally come out as you release abdominal tension.

2. Get ready to laugh! Placing your feet firmly on the ground, bend your knees deeply until you are squatting in a birth position. Place your elbows on your knees to steady yourself. Take a deep breath, filling your rib cage with air; then, pushing down with your elbows, let out a big belly laugh: Ha-Ha-Ha! Repeat until your abdomen feels lighter, more open.

These exercises loosen your breathing. The second exercise often opens a Pandora's Box of laughter. Some of us have years of laughter packed inside us waiting to spring forth. Write a short piece about laughter. It could be a humorous dialogue, or a quick story, or a moment that forms itself into poetry. Whatever form your writing takes, let it bend in an untried direction. Let it expand its possibilities to fit the space you have just made for it in your body.

WHILE WAITING ON THE MUSE, ANIMATE THE BODY

Sometimes the truth depends on a walk around the lake.

—Wallace Stevens

Arrange whatever pieces come your way.

—Virginia Woolf

Some of us turn gray waiting for the Muse to descend on us. When lightning finally strikes, we're happy to write. But what do we do in the meantime? Clean the house? Drive around? Watch television? Talk?

If you're committed to your writing, you can't wait for a chariot to drop *War and Peace* at the doorstep. You must chase after the words like a jilted lover. You must pine after them, adore them. If waiting is involved, then wait for them artfully, playfully. Don't become stagnant in your writing, for when the body gets stuck, it stops breathing fully. And the breath is the Source of your words.

When the Muse does not descend willingly, you must descend into your body. You can walk or jump or run, or move in whatever way brings you back to your physical self. Movement begets movement: as the heart pumps the lifeblood through your veins, so your pen will begin pumping words. As your knees bend to accommodate the slopes and dips of hills and trails, so will your language take on the shape of your interior landscape—rushing forth like a wild river, or stilling itself like a lonely mountain.

Why sit staring at a blank page or a computer screen? Dance, don't sit! Consider the possibility that your body may be "too full" of information to put it all down on paper. Movement has a cleansing, clarifying effect. Every writer I know has some ritual for emptying the body: one runs long distances, one practices Tai Chi, one digs in the garden, one cranks up the stereo and jigs to Irish folk music.

You can go outside to get back inside. Spend a good long time looking at the sun or the moon. There's more in those orbs than you'll ever find orbiting the empty page. Don't listen to the voice in you that says you're not a "serious" writer if you're concentrating on the stars instead of stapling down sentences. Remember your promise to yourself to give up being "serious." Remember that you're going to exchange that posture for a soulful wildness, for the fun of body and beauty.

Many will say this way of inviting inspiration is too romantic, that great writing requires sitting, thinking, worrying, suffering. Fine. There's room for all that, if you *must*. But most of us refuse to understand that really good writing comes as a gift, and that thinking hard and staring may not be necessary at all. If we want to write from the body, we must free the body to move about. In the end, we'll know if we've been successful, by whether our body resonates to the words we've written.

Yes, we have to prepare and practice, research and reconstruct. But patience with ourselves, and a willingness to wander awhile, is often more valuable that any expertise we may gather. If we are to respect the timing of the writing process, its incalculable rhythms, we have to be willing to spend a fair amount of time walking and listening to the still, small voices within. There's no risk or beauty in forcing ourselves to sit and produce a dry essay on our stuckness. Why waste our time?

If the Muse is asleep, then wake up your body with exercise, attention, healthful food, with a long walk through the woods. Dance, drum, sing, shout, scream, but don't sit still expecting "something to come to you." Go out into an open field, or take a seat on a patch of grass for a while, and discover what you need to return to your writing table. Your body knows what you need. And it isn't going to produce one inspired word until it gets it.

Here's an exercise: Try any kind of movement you enjoy—walk with a brisk step, run somewhere, dance freely to some favorite music, swim a few laps, whatever your body likes. While you're moving, let songs and scenes, memories, emotions, sentences and paragraphs, poems, even unintelligible sounds, arise inside you as you move. Listen attentively, and with love. Trust that when you return to your desk, you'll remember the essentials. When you arrive home, whatever remains in your memory is a gift of the Muse. Accept it and enjoy it, swim in it as you would an early-morning dream. When you awaken, the details you remember are yours.

Body Work:
The Pelvic Area

The pelvic region is the home of your sense of survival, and your creativity/sexuality. When you feel fear or feel pressure to perform, you may tighten up the pelvic region. You can't write wildly without the help of this part of your body.

I suggest having someone read the following exercise to you as you do it, or making an audiotape of the instructions so that you can follow along without referring to the text.

To free up the pelvic area, stand with your feet hip-distance apart and firmly planted on the ground, knees slightly bent. Allow your spine to softly stretch and lengthen. Feel the crown of your head rising as if attached to a string. Allow your chin to drop slightly. Placing your hands on your hips, begin to rotate the hips full circle—clockwise, then counterclockwise, then clockwise again. Remember to let your knees stay unlocked and loose as you move. This should be fun! It's great if you want to include music. Even better if you can let yourself make some "yippee!" sounds to go with this movement. Challenge yourself to feel the wildness of your body. Let yourself shout for joy. At first it may feel odd to do this, but that's only because your body has had more practice expressing negativities than expressing its natural bliss. But that joy is there. I promise.

FINDING YOUR
VOICE

---

*My heart is inditing a good matter: I speak of the things
which I have made touching the King: my tongue is the pen
of a ready writer.*

—Psalms 45:1

So now you know how to move; if you've tried some of the
exercises, you believe in movement. You're not taking yourself
or the critics too seriously, you've stopped listening too closely
to the Inner Critic, and you're willing to let out the sighs, the
tears, the terror and the ecstasy. Your "voice" is finally ready
to be heard. Now that you've thawed your frozen feelings, the
Voice for which you have searched so deeply is about to speak.

A writer's authentic "voice" is always recognizable because
it carries the ring of truth. Like singers, we know when we're
"in voice," and when we're not. I wish I could tell you more.
I wish I could say, "First you read Chaucer, then you do sixteen

push-ups to a John Philip Sousa march, then your voice will speak." But the truth is that the path to finding the voice is the same path we take all our lives to find our true Self. It happens gradually.

Regaining your natural sense of breath and movement by doing the exercises you've done so far is a good beginning. If you have accepted the challenge of this book, and tried the movements and body work recommended here, you will have made some breakthroughs. You will have discovered information through "body wisdom" that you would not have discovered in any other way. That information may seem at first to lead you down conflicting inner roads. Your responses to what you've found may range from deciding you want to interview everyone in your family, to escaping to the mountains for a month to write a novel, to renewing your interest in science, to exploring possibilities that seem to have nothing whatsoever to do with writing. Whatever your response, you have embarked on the journey toward your voice. And since the two journeys—the one to your voice as a writer, and the one to the Voice of your true Self—are the same, you will be seeking something very important indeed.

The "voice" of a writer often shows up in the writing as mirroring his or her speech patterns. But it's more than that. It's the mirror of who we are, all the inflections and articulations of our true nature. So, like us, it wears many faces. Just as our speaking voice sometimes leaps and shouts, sometimes chokes on tears, sometimes tiptoes on a whisper, so our writing voice echoes our different states of being. The voice in this poem whispers:

MAGIC STORY FOR
FALLING ASLEEP

*When the last giant came out of his cave
and his bones turned into the mountain*

115

and his clothes turned into the flowers,

nothing was left but his tooth
which my dad took home in his truck
which my granddad carved into a bed

which my mom tucks me into at night
when I dream of the last giant
when I fall asleep on the mountain.

—Nancy Willard

The voice of this poem glides along, speaking like a sleepy child. The lines have a lulling quality: they stretch out in long, relaxed breaths of equal length, and lay themselves down quietly. We believe this voice because we have felt its rhythms in our own bodies as we fall asleep. It is not a "risky" or turbulent poem, but its voice is true.

The voice in the novel excerpt below also alludes to night and bedtime, but its voice is wild with unrest. The voice is true to the narrator's mental turbulence:

> . . . if Mother was up we always began by playing on the porch until she said we were making too much noise, then we went out and played under the wistaria frame.
>
> This was where I saw the river for the last time this morning, about here. I could feel water beyond the twilight, smell. When it bloomed in the spring and it rained the smell was everywhere you didn't notice it so much at other times but when it rained the smell began to come into the house at twilight either it would rain more at twilight or there was something in the light itself but it always smelled strongest then until I would lie in bed thinking when will it stop when will it stop. The draft in the door smelled of water, a damp steady breath. Sometimes I could put myself to sleep saying that over and over until after the honeysuckle got all mixed up in it the

whole thing came to symbolise night and unrest I seemed to be lying neither asleep nor awake looking down a long corridor of grey halflight where all stable things had become shadowy paradoxical all I had done shadows all I had felt suffered taking visible form antic and perverse mocking without relevance inherent themselves with the denial of the significance they should have affirmed thinking I was I was not who was not was not who.

In this passage from Faulkner's *The Sound and the Fury*, Quentin's internal voice reports his reverie breathlessly, or at times in a halting confusion, straining against an emotional tidal wave. It is a voice that builds in intensity, choking back angry tears.

Their tones are very different, yet both pieces ring true; both are "in voice."

When we are "in voice" we speak plainly, from the heart. When I am being less than authentic, my vocal cords contract and I speak in a higher voice. When I'm being truthful, then, as Rumi wrote, "I speak the low tones of thunder." The same thing takes place in our writing. Often the true voice emerges only after a false voice has had its long say, and is silenced by exhaustion. And our true voice can contain many voices. It is not restricted to the speech patterns of our particular personality, because the true Voice is that of the inner Self. It is Everyvoice. As Gary Snyder once said in an interview, ". . . a great poet does not express his or her self; he expresses all of our selves. . . . you have to go beyond your own self."

Here is a poem by W. S. Merwin. Because it is a conversation, this poem speaks in the (quite distinctive) voice of the poet as well as in the voice of his friend. At one point the poet interrupts his friend, but shortly the poet's voice gives way to his friend's need to speak. The poet-speaker, the "I," becomes primarily a listener, and begins to learn something about himself and his own father's death. As the poet's "personality voice" fades and gives way to the voice of his friend, a greater Voice rises out of the poem's conversation. In the last four lines, the friend's voice becomes Everyvoice, speaking for everyone who has ever loved someone and failed them, and later felt deep regret:

YESTERDAY

My friend says I was not a good son
you understand
I say yes I understand

he says I did not go
to see my parents very often you know
and I say yes I know

even when I was living in the same city he says
maybe I would go there once
a month or maybe even less
I say oh yes

he says the last time I went to see my father
I say the last time I saw my father

he says the last time I saw my father
he was asking me about my life
how I was making out and he
went into the next room
to get something to give me

oh I say
feeling again the cold
of my father's hand the last time

he says and my father turned
in the doorway and saw me
look at my wristwatch and he
said you know I would like you to stay
and talk with me

118

oh yes I say

but if you are busy he said
I don't want you to feel that you
have to
just because I'm here

I say nothing

he says my father
said maybe
you have important work you are doing
or maybe you should be seeing
somebody I don't want to keep you

I look out the window
my friend is older than I am
he says and I told my father it was so
and I got up and left him then
you know

though there was nowhere I had to go
and nothing I had to do

The greater Voice occurs naturally, when we are off-guard, writing along with a certain simplicity of mind. We can prepare ourselves for the time of writing by reading the works of inspired writers, by honing our craft, but when the time comes to write, we must forget all that and just move forward, letting the ink run its own course.

You know you're not writing "in voice" when the words stick, when they don't flow easily. When I write, it's easy to tell when I've stopped simply speaking and started complicatedly thinking: I begin crossing out, coming up with "better" words, "more interesting" phrases. I'm dressing up the language before it's even been born. I look at the page and it's dark—with scratching scrawls and tiny phrases curling in on themselves where I ran out of room in the margin. I stopped creating and started revising. The two can't go on at the same time.

Do your best to stay in the body. Honor the words that come, at the times they want to come, in the way that they want to be said. Put aside your agendas and let the words roll themselves into the shapes they were meant to assume. You may begin with an agenda—"This is what I'm going to say"— but you must be willing to surrender it at a moment's notice, whenever the words bend in a new direction. The process is often hit-and-miss. You won't always love the product. But, just as living from your truth gradually bears the amazing fruit of Self-insight and spiritual discovery, remaining true to your writing voice provides its own built-in reward: you write freely, happily.

Many voices: By learning about some of the characters in which our Voice may speak, we begin to see new avenues for going deeper in our writing, and into our Self. Below are four exercises to reacquaint you with your many voices. Give yourself enough time to dream, to write, and to feel the emotions that arise from this process.

Have a pen or pencil and paper ready before you begin, and start by breathing deeply and fully. There's no rush. This is discovery time, island time.

1. Close your eyes and take a deep breath. Remember a time when you were small, when everything around you was large—the people, the furniture, the world. Breathing deeply, listen awhile. Go inside your child self and say the words that come from that voice. Then write them down, taking as much time as you need.

2. Repeat the above exercise, imagining yourself in your adolescent years. Go inside and reacquaint yourself with the sights and sounds and feelings of your life at age fourteen or fifteen. Then find the words of that voice, and record them.

3. Repeat the same exercise with yourself as an adult. Go deep inside and, breathing deeply, write the words of your voice today.

4. Go inside one last time. Find in yourself the person you are becoming—the kinder, wiser you. Feel that part of you deep in your being. Breathe in and out of that future body, and say and write the words of that voice-to-come.

When you have written in all of these voices, go back and read the words of each of them. Within the many, can you hear the one Voice, the Everyvoice? At this point, you may want to write again from this more expanded perspective.

Body Work:
The Throat

The throat is a harbor for much that we have left unsaid and unfelt in our lives, and for the personal power of the Voice we have yet to claim. Often our truth "sticks in our throat," or we feel "choked up," unable to say the words trapped in our bodies. Our throat is knotted with unspoken dreams and un-cried tears. Here is a way to break through those blocks, those "lumps in the throat": Placing a pillow close to your face, focus on the energy knotted up in the throat area. Yell and shout from deep in your belly if you need to, sending all that blocked energy out of your throat. Your voice will be tired after doing this, so let it rest. After about an hour, your vocal cords will relax and your voice will sound lower. After doing this exercise a number of times as needed (whenever you hear the pitch of your voice rising, or feel your throat tightening up), the pitch of your voice may lower itself by as much as an entire octave. You will also notice a new power in your voice, and in your words, both spoken and written.

After doing the exercise above to open the throat area, go to a piece of writing that's been incubating for a while. Every one of us has the rough sketch for a story, a diary entry we stopped midflow, or a half-finished letter. Find the work that you have left unfinished, and finish it.

ANSWERS
FROM THE
BODY

In the Writing from the Body workshop, I receive questions of all kinds, from all kinds of writers. In the following examples I have tried to encapsulate some common concerns, and to suggest how writing from the body can be directly applied to specific writing problems.

I've been working on a novel for two years. I've come a long way in developing the plot, but it has begun to shift, and I'm not sure where it's going. The main male character has just met "another woman," and try as I may to write him back toward the heroine, it doesn't work. He won't have anything to do with her. How can I "write from the body" to solve this problem?

Aristotle said that "plot is character." When you have difficulty knowing what a character should do next, or feeling affection for a character, let the plot itself propel the body of that character into action. Whatever your character does next is *who he is*. Look for the physical details—does he walk around wringing his hands? Does he slam the door on his way out of the room? Let the character's body move around in the story. That will move the plot.

Exercise to get the character moving: Place yourself in a close approximation of your character's physical situation. Or place your father or mother there, or a good friend. What would your father do next? or your sister? Think of how you've seen people move and behave in this situation.

You must rely on actual movement to create fictional movement. The difference between "head writing" and "body writing" is going into the storehouse of your body knowledge to find the *true* movement, rather than inventing it.

As a female journalist, I'm especially drawn to subjects involving women's issues. I've been working on a piece about three young Israeli women who grew up in settlements in the Gaza Strip. I find I'm so emotionally close to the story now that I'm not sure whether the writing is any good. I'm so affected by the struggles and the losses of these women that I feel I'm losing my perspective. Can I use writing from the body to clarify my approach?

Yes. This dilemma is asking you to deal with your own interior struggles and the losses you've accrued over your lifetime. Many people will weep for lives not their own, but cannot cry over the losses they have lived. How do you relate to these women's losses? In what way does their grief echo your own, either in the recent or distant past? To write about their struggles in a way that will best serve the truth, you must first deal with your own struggles, your own losses.

Exercise: Consider each woman individually. Of whom does she remind you? In what way are her difficulties like your own? You may not ever have come home to a bombed-out apartment, but have you ever been robbed or cheated? Literally *or* figuratively? Consider the women as a group. What qualities do they possess as a group that remind you of groups you belong to? If you don't find any resemblances, say to yourself this sentence: "My government has never oppressed me as a woman." Just try that on emotionally. You must feel your own oppression first, get to the catharsis that's coming from your own life experience, before you can report *from your body, from your truth*, about other women's lives. Aristotle told us that this was the purpose of all art—to effect a cultural or individual catharsis.

I've always trusted my own writing instincts. I follow my impulses. I feel confident about how to craft a piece once it's in shape for revision. But what do you do when your impulses lead you astray? For the first time lately, I feel I have nothing to write about. I seem to reject anything I think of, as soon as it occurs to me. Is there an exercise I could do to break out of this? I feel I'm losing ground.

When you say, "I reject anything I think of," that tells you to stop thinking so hard. Sometimes we think too much. The way through is to let the body *feel* its way into the right subject. Our prayer to the Muse should be "Teach us to think and not to think," a variation on T. S. Eliot's "Teach me to care and not to care." We need not to think and reject, but to feel and write.

Here's an exercise: As fast as you can, write down everything you've considered writing about lately—all the ideas you've been rejecting. Then devote one writing period (thirty minutes to an hour) to writing about one of those subjects. You can do one subject a day like this, until clarity comes.

Then write about a time when you tried to start something and you were prevented from finishing it. Maybe there was a time when you were working on a project and someone interjected a negative opinion before you had conceived the whole picture—something that was interrupted in its infancy. The cocoon was slit. Premature assessment can kill creativity. Write about how that felt; report what goes on in your body while you write.

I write plays. I have been wringing my hands over this one section of dialogue for weeks, and nothing's happening. Everything I write feels phony; I just don't believe the words I'm putting into the character's mouths. Does writing from the body address this problem?

I want you to try an exercise. Divide a sheet of paper into two columns. In one column, list all the people who have spoken to you in a phony way. And in the other column, write down why you think they may have been speaking inauthentically. Turn the paper over and, once again, divide it into two columns. In one, briefly write down memories of recent conversations you've had in which you felt that *your own* words were phony. Then, for each situation, write down what kept you from being authentic. This exercise will help you discover whether blocks in your own body are preventing you from writing straightforwardly.

But check your motives. Do you want these characters to sound *real*, or do you want them to sound *correct*? Consider that your characters may be only exhibiting your Shadow self. Like you, they have a right to it. To be authentic characters, they would have to exhibit elements of the Shadow in their makeup. If this rings true to you, then don't edit so much what your characters are saying. Let them speak freely. Let them move around. They may be working their way toward new growth, new content, interesting leaps, surprises!

Is it possible to write too much? I've always kept a diary. I write in it almost every night. During the day I find myself thinking, "This will be great for my journal." Is there anything wrong with this? Am I becoming a hermit?

Journal writing is self-reflective. Even the greatest journal writers manage to keep contact with the outside world. Thoreau, for example. Even during his time at Walden Pond, he visited with his mother nearly every day.

You can actually use your journal to process the fear of being alone. Let the journal be the receptacle for that fear—write about it. Then you'll be likely to use it as a vehicle to come closer to others. This fear you're articulating is often the very thing that keeps us alone. In your journal, give free rein to your fears of being left alone. The key is to be completely candid in your journal. Say *everything*. Don't edit. Many of us don't like to admit it, but we sometimes edit what we write in our journals, out of fear of what people might read about us in our absence. We imagine they might find our journal after our death, or that someone might snoop through our things and read our secrets. Whatever your fears, write openly. Don't imprison your words. You can always destroy certain pages of your journal later, if you need to do that.

I know I'm a good writer, and that I'm able to articulate my ideas clearly. But it's a dry process for me. I do it by the numbers. I work in the world of business, so I have to maintain a certain equanimity, a certain decorum. How can I liven up my writing without losing clarity and professionalism?

Even in the world of business, the ones most admired are those fearless enough to say what must be said. Boldness is almost always appreciated. Brashness, of course, is not. Even in your business writing, risk being bold. Say what needs to be said, without reservation.

Ask yourself, "Would I be willing to live meekly?" The Bible says, "The meek shall inherit the earth," but it doesn't say in what condition it will be when they inherit it.

Here's an exercise: In the privacy of your first draft, treat your subject as boldly, as flamboyantly, and as dramatically as you possibly can. Really stretch yourself. Then, in your second and third drafts, you can adjust it down a notch for your business public. But in that first draft, exaggerate, exaggerate, exaggerate! Later you can go in and make sure you dotted all your "i's." This is one way to get the lively phrases to appear on the page. And you won't just get lively prose; you can discover new content, new ideas through writing with complete abandon in your first draft. If you leave in some of the juicy stuff, you may feel uneasy the first time you reveal your vibrant writing to your peers. Nora Ephron once wrote that her second husband would erase all his appointments at the end of the year so that he wouldn't feel he was so busy! You can always go back and delete the exciting parts of your writing, so that no one will guess how interesting you are!

All writing involves an element of risk.

I write in my journal in a "stream-of-consciousness" fashion. But most of what I write seems all jumbled up and unclear. How could writing from the body help me get clear about what I'm saying?

You're writing breathlessly, as though you're chasing down the words. Stream-of-consciousness writing doesn't always make rational sense when we read it later, though as a process it can be helpful. You get writing of quality from deepening the quality of your feeling.

Exercise: Before putting pen to paper, take ten deep, slow cycles of breath. Rather than writing so quickly, write only a sentence or two, then stop. Take a deep, full, luxurious breath, and let it out. Then write a sentence or two more, and stop for another deep breath. Try this for a while to break your body's pattern of rushing headlong to grab the words before they get away.

The words are chasing *you*. Slow down so that you can be caught.

In my journal writing, I often find myself slipping from personal narrative into a sort of personal myth or fable or fairy tale. These myths seem to me highly symbolic, but after a point I can no longer decipher the symbols. Can writing from the body help me interpret the symbolism in these personal "mythical" stories?

Most people don't spend enough *time* with their personal symbols, in either their dreams or their lives. The body moves more slowly, more primally. The brain is the one easily bored, the one that wants to get on with it. It's hard to bore the body.

Slow down. Wrestle with each symbol. Let the symbol deepen and transmute itself over the course of a few days.

I have a symbol like this, a recurring image of a prison. I respond to it by staying with that prison image. I don't move on to the next thing, and the next, like the Puer, the eternal boy or Flying Boy. Instead, I've read all I can about prisons. I've painted pictures of prisons. I've written in my journal about prisons, and the various ideas and associations I have about imprisonment. I keep plumbing the depths of that symbol's meaning for me. By staying with that one symbol, I get more information than if I tried to go after all of them at once. Depth yields multiplicity. A symbol is a depth marker. It tells you where to dive. It looks simple on the surface, but once you get underneath it, a vast world of multiple meanings appears before you.

You have to stay with each symbol until it's finished with you. Once the symbol has delivered its message, it stops appearing in your dreams and in your writing. Only the symbol knows its shelf life.

Look for the most potent symbols, those that recur, those that resonate in your body, those that carry an emotional charge for you. Pick up the heaviest ones first.

GOODBYE AND
GOOD WRITING!

If you've sampled each of the writing exercises in this book, you're ready to hear and see what further creations wait inside you. Dreaming has been replaced by doing. You're willing to feel your life in every pore. Instead of dining on distance every evening, you'll be writing words to fill your hungry soul. You will come home, word by word, to your true Self and Voice. As part of the natural course of things, you will also grow closer to the people who love and support your creativity.

Instead of writing from the head you'll write from your bones, from your gut, from your depth. And though sometimes you may still feel afraid when confronted with the Shadow in your writing, you'll be able to let the fear pass through your body without stopping. You'll let it move through your arms and out of your pen. The fear of offending someone, of not getting your work published, can be danced out, screamed out, pushed out by muscle and will. A thrill of energy will revitalize every organ and limb as you break open the lies that have bound you to a fantasy audience. By breaking through those unreal barriers to your truth, you will have made the most important discovery of your writing life.

Your audience is you. You are completely free to create for yourself, for the pure delight you feel in writing. You may continue to write only in private—wonderful. Enjoy. Or you may seek to publish your finished work. If you do publish, you'll still be singing your truth long after the royalty checks appear. Now that you've worked so diligently to find and claim it, promise yourself not to let your Voice disappear. Go the way of Whitman: allow yourself to be transformed by your writing, and "sing the body electric." Through the process of pouring out your truth, you'll be joining the voices of angels, and you'll put your inner demons on notice that their days are numbered.

Dance with your writing, belt out sentences that satisfy your soul. Write from your body, and your writing will find its own body. And, as surely as one breath follows another, the rift between mind and heart will begin to mend. You will be armed with the conviction that can come only through surrender to the wild mysteries of language, and no one will ever be able to silence you again.

> *Let knowledge grow from more to more,*
> *But more of reverence in us dwell,*
> *That mind and soul, according well,*
> *May make one music as before.*

—Alfred, Lord Tennyson

> *Someone who goes with half a loaf of bread*
> *to a small place that fits like a nest around him,*

someone who wants no more, who's not himself
longed for by anyone else,

He is a letter to everyone. You open it.
It says, Live.

—Rumi
   translated by John Moyne and Coleman Barks

AUTHOR'S NOTE

We think and name in one world,
we live and feel in another.

—Marcel Proust

Early on, I wanted to write more than anything. I was told that I couldn't write. I was ill prepared to go against the criticism and negativity I received, especially in college. On one paper I submitted, a professor wrote, "I can't read or understand your writing." But somehow I managed to get through undergraduate school after two attempts (after the first, they politely invited me to leave with a .02 grade-point average). I went out into the Real World for a while and decided to go back and try again. I did well the second go-round, though no one but my friend Mrs. Timmons thought I had a chance at writing anything that anyone else would want to read.

From there I went to graduate school, where writing was necessary but not often very moving. We weren't exactly "singing the body electric." We celebrated the intellect alone, the pointed critique of Pure Reason. I struggled through two years and received a master's degree, thanking God that I had escaped having to write a thesis.

From there I reluctantly sought a Ph.D. at the University of Texas, where my desire (if not my ability) to write increased. Somehow I managed to talk my way through my courses, writing about half of what is usually required. Finally, after five years of graduate coursework, and after teaching in the American studies, religious studies, and English departments for twelve years, I still couldn't write with any degree of confidence.

I tried everything. I penned country/rock songs, poetry, journalistic prose, but nothing I wrote excited me, and I knew it wasn't going to excite any reader, much less a publisher.

When the time came to write the dreaded dissertation, I took off a semester and headed south to Mexico, carrying with me three hundred dollars and a stack of books on writing, hoping I'd be able to absorb their wisdom by osmosis.

I returned from Mexico with amebic dysentery, hardly able to stand, and with a dissertation coming due. I prayed for the Second Coming, and watched as the love of my youth, Laural, left our relationship, a departure which left me unable to *think* myself out of the problem. I could not reason the pain away, though I made earnest attempts to numb it and drown it. This grief kept resurrecting itself, in concert with my powerful desire to write.

Two sensitive professors had been attempting to guide me through the "mind field" of dissertation writing without the loss of the little sanity I still possessed. I began writing a "scholarly" treatise on Robert Bly, C. G. Jung, and the Men's Movement—a lot of mental masturbation. With every new draft of the first chapter, my professors would see that gaping wound staring out from the pages—my despair over Laural's leaving, and a life I was living poorly. Both Betty Sue Flowers and Bill Stott would dig through the mounds of pontification, pounce on that particle of truth, and say, "We want more of this."

After several months, both teachers asked me in their own ways why I didn't take a break from the dissertation and deal in print with my breakup with Laural. Both of them admitted to recognizing bits and pieces of their own stories in mine, whenever I had been bold enough to write the truth. I kept trying to explain to those learned and caring people that telling my story would not get me what I needed. Clearly, writing about breaking up with Laural would not earn a Ph.D., the essential element in my plan to prove to my father that I was smarter than he was.

But the grief was so deep and the despair so wide that I really didn't have much choice. Either I would go into the writing through the doorway of my body, or I would have to go on numbing my body and my pain with alcohol, women, work, and degrees. With much help and support, I was eventually able to drop into my body—a descent that led straight into my past. I met not only the dark memories lodged for years in my back, my buttocks, my chest, arms, legs, and throat, but in those aching corners I also found my passion: writing from the body.

Although such writing was not plentiful among the work I had studied, I had managed to discover Whitman, Thoreau, Steinbeck, Bly, and a few others who wrote from the depths. The rest of what I found had left me cold and dry, just as I had left Laural's house on many a hot summer night.

When at last I had given up "what I was supposed to do" and "how I was supposed to do it," I transferred my body's story onto paper. I gave it to my professors and they blessed it: one with tears, one with a smile. Both congratulated me on being able to do what most graduate students shrink from—telling the truth no matter what the outcome.

Bill Stott said, "In your truth I see some of my own, and that's what every reader wants to find." Now, nine years later, 250,000 people have bought that book, which Bill and I and my agent and a number of publishers had said would never get into print. *The Flying Boy* has been translated into four languages and led to the writing of six more books. I never received my Ph.D., but I have never since deserted my body. Though I still tend to live in my head a good deal of the time, I know, feel, and trust that my best writing, and yours, comes when the whole body is involved—not just the brain, but the Big Picture of Mind/Body/Soul that we really are.

I sent out the manuscript of *The Flying Boy* to more than two dozen publishers, and all of them rejected it. Two responded that if I would be willing to rewrite the entire book, making it less personal and more "how-to," they'd be glad to take a second look. All the others said in various ways that no one would want to read the painful autobiography of an unknown. They didn't think anyone would want to hear my truth. My friends John Hunger and Allen Maurer believed in that truth, believed in me so much that they put up the money, and we published it ourselves.

To write *The Flying Boy*, I found *myself first*. I entered the pain I had avoided all my life, found my truth, and put it on paper. Publishing came much later.

To tell that story, I took back my own voice—the Alabama voice I had rejected. And in doing so I found that greater Voice, the one so many readers responded to. All I had wanted was to tell the truth, and stop pretending. Because that writing changed me, today I agree with Brenda Ueland that "no writing is a waste of time. . . . With every sentence you write, you have learned something. It has done you good."

It is my hope that what is written here has enlivened you, and will continue to reveal new riches in your own writing, as you move through your fears to claim your true voice.

POSTSCRIPT

Writing is a solitary endeavor. In many ways, that solitude is what attracted me to writing in the first place. I seem to feel most comfortable when I'm alone. Being in large groups frankly scares me. But giving up not the solitude, but the desert of isolation I had built around my writing, has turned out to be one of the greatest stretching acts I've performed during my writing life. In this book I've reaped great benefits from joining my talents with those of Ceci Miller-Kritsberg.

I had written two other books with my friend Bill Stott, but in those books I gave him my ideas, and he did most of the writing himself. By this method we produced two books

I'm very proud of: *Recovery: Plain and Simple* and *Facing the Fire: Experiencing and Expressing Anger Appropriately*. At first I contracted to write this book alone. But, as often happens, Fate had other ideas.

In short, I ended up inviting Ceci Miller-Kritsberg to work with me on this project. First she was to work with me in an editorial capacity, but that evolved into my gathering the courage to ask her to write this book with me. It wasn't easy! I'm still actively working on my ability to trust, and my ease in this area has increased dramatically since Ceci and I began working together.

When Ceci and I began seriously exploring the possibility of doing this book as a team, I realized with new clarity that I could, in fact, write the book by myself. I had written enough books that way before. But it also became clear that I didn't *have* to write the book alone and, to my surprise, I found that I really didn't *want* to do it alone.

I knew that Ceci's contribution would greatly improve the quality and depth of the book. She brought to the project a rich and varied background as a poet and writer, teacher, counselor, and workshop presenter. And I knew that I wanted this book to touch as many writers and nonwriters as possible, because I believe so deeply in the material we've presented, having taught it in workshops and seen the immediate positive results.

Ceci's background frankly impressed me. She had received her M.F.A. from this nation's premier writing institution, the University of Iowa Writers' Workshop, had studied with Donald Justice, Marvin Bell, and others, and had a number of creative writing awards and publications to her credit. All this, together with her obvious passion for the written word as it emanates from the body, and her natural compassion for those struggling with their own creative process, would blend beautifully with my own ideas and insights, training, and love of writing that touches both body and soul.

So I took a few days' worth of deep breaths, then asked Ceci to join me—and the book and I are both better off for my decision. Many of the exercises, ideas, and rich prose are hers, and I'm happy to say that today I still trust that you've had a finer reading experience thanks to her part in this book. Most of all I trust that, if you take what we've offered here, you will move closer to creating what you really want, both in your writing and in the rest of your life.

BOOKS ON WRITING
I RECOMMEND

Walking on Alligators, Susan Shaughnessy, HarperSanFrancisco, 1993.
If You Want to Write, Brenda Ueland, Graywolf Press, 1987.
Writing Down the Bones, Natalie Goldberg, Shambhala Publications Inc., 1986.
The Art of Writing, Lu Chi, Milkweed Editions, 1991.
Writing the Natural Way, Gabriele Lusser Rico, J.P. Tarcher, Inc., 1983.
Wild Mind: Living the Writer's Life, Natalie Goldberg, Bantam New Age Books, 1990.
Writing With Power, Peter Elbow, Oxford University Press, 1981.
Writing Past Dark, Bonnie Friedman, HarperCollins Publishers, Inc., 1993.
Writing for Your Life, Deena Metzger, HarperSanFrancisco, 1992.
Write to the Point, Bill Stott, Columbia University Press, New York, 1991.
The Writing Life, Annie Dillard, HarperPerennial, 1990.
Creative Writing, Dianne Doubtfire, Hodder and Stoughton, 1993.
Zen in the Art of Writing, Ray Bradbury, Joshua Odell Editions, Capra Press, 1990.
Long Quiet Highway, Natalie Goldberg, Bantam Books, 1993.
How to Write Like a Pro, Barry Tarshis, Plume, 1982.

BIBLIOGRAPHY

Bachelard, Gaston. *The Poetics of Reverie: Childhood, Language and the Cosmos*. Boston: Beacon Press, 1969.

Barks, Coleman. "On Resurrection Day," *This Longing: Versions of Rumi*. [pub. data TK]

Bell, Marvin. "What They Do To You in Distant Places," *The Iris of Creation*. Port Townsend, WA: Copper Canyon Press, 1990.

Bly, Robert, comp. *Lorca and Jimenez: Selected Poems*. Boston: Beacon Press, 1973.

Bly, Robert, comp. *Neruda & Vallejo: Selected Poems*. Boston: Beacon Press, 1971.

Bly, Robert, "Warning to the Reader," *What Have I Ever Lost By Dying?: Collected Prose Poems*. New York: HarperCollins, 1992.

Bly, Robert. "The Jar With the Dry Rim," *When Grapes Turn to Wine: Versions of Rumi*. Cambridge: Yellow Moon Press, 1986.

Bode, Richard. *First You Have to Row a Little Boat: Reflections on Life & Living*. New York: Warner Books, 1993.

Bradbury, Ray. *Zen in the Art of Writing*. Santa Barbara, California: Joshua Odell Editions, 1990.

Brown, Rita Mae. *Wish You Were Here*. New York: Bantam Books/CrimeLine, 1990.

Chinen, Alan. *Once Upon a Midlife: Classic Stories and Mythic Tales to Illuminate the Middle Years*. Los Angeles: Jeremy P. Tarcher, 1992.

Dillard, Annie. *Living By Fiction*. New York: Harper & Row, 1982.

Dillard, Annie. *The Writing Life*. New York: Harper & Row, 1989.

Ellison, Ralph. *Invisible Man*. New York: Modern Library, 1992.

Faulkner, William. *The Sound and the Fury*. New York: Random House, 1956.

Flagg, Fannie. *Fried Green Tomatoes at the Whistle Stop Cafe*. New York: Random House, 1987.

Friedman, Bonnie. *Writing Past Dark: Envy, Fear, Distraction, and Other Dilemmas in the Writer's Life*. New York: HarperCollins Publishers, 1993.

Gentry, Marshall Brue and Stull, William L., eds. *Conversations with Raymond Carver*. Jackson: University Press of Mississippi, 1990.

Gibbons, Reginald, ed. "The Duende: Theory and Divertissement" by Federico García Lorca and "Projective Verse and the Practice" by William Carlos Williams, *The Poet's Work*. Boston: Houghton Mifflin Co., 1979.

Goldberg, Natalie. *Writing Down the Bones*. Boston: Shambhala Lion Editions, 1989.

Johnson, Robert A. *Owning Your Own Shadow: Understanding the Dark Side of the Psyche*. San Francisco: HarperSanFrancisco, 1991.

Joyce, James. *Ulysses*. ed. Hans Walter Gabler. New York: Random House, 1986.

Kinnell, Galway. "The Still Time," *Mortal Acts, Mortal Words*. Boston: Houghton Mifflin Co., 1980.

Knight, Etheridge. "Belly Song," and "Feeling Fucked Up," *Born of a Woman*. Boston: Houghton Mifflin Co., 1980.

Kundera, Milan. *The Art of the Novel*. New York: Grove Press, 1986.

Merwin, W. S. "Yesterday," *Opening the Hand*. New York: Atheneum, 1983.

Metzger, Deena. *Writing for Your Life: A Guide and Companion to the Inner Worlds*. New York: HarperCollins Publishers, 1992.

Moyne, John and Barks, Coleman. *Open Secret: Versions of Rumi*. Putney, VT: Threshold Books, 1984.

Oates, Joyce Carol. "Slow," *The Assignation: Stories*. New York: Ecco Press, 1988.

Phillips, Jayne Anne. "Blind Girls," *Black Tickets*. New York: Delta, 1984.

Plimpton, George, ed. *Women Writers at Work: The Paris Review Interviews*. New York: Penguin, 1989.

Roethke, Theodore. "In a Dark Time," *The Far Field*. Garden City, New York: Anchor Books (Doubleday), 1971.

Scully, James. "Notes on the Art of Poetry" by Dylan Thomas, *Modern Poetics*. New York: McGraw-Hill, 1965.

Seibles, Timothy. "The Body Knew," *Body Moves*. San Antonio: Corona Publishing Co., 1988.

Stafford, William. *The Darkness Around Us Is Deep*, ed. Robert Bly. New York: HarperPerennial, 1993.

Stafford, William. *Writing the Australian Crawl.* Ann Arbor: The University of Michigan Press, 1982.

Transtromer, Tomas. "From March '79" trans. John F. Deane, *Selected Poems 1954–1986.* ed. Robert Hass. New York: Ecco Press, 1987.

Ueland, Brenda. *If You Want To Write.* St. Paul: Graywolf Press, 1987.

Waller, Robert James. *The Bridges of Madison County.* New York: Warner Books, 1992.

Welty, Eudora. "Sir Rabbit," *Collected Stories of Eudora Welty.* Harcourt, Brace Jovanovich, 1982.

Willard, Nancy. "Magic Story for Falling Asleep," *Water Walker.* New York: Knopf, 1989.

Williams, William Carlos. "Danse Russe," *The Collected Poems of William Carlos Williams.* New York: New Directions, 1988.

Woodman, Marion with Kate Dawson; Mary Hamilton and Rita Greer Allen. *Leaving My Father's House: A Journey to Conscious Femininity.* Boston: Shambhala Press, 1992.

Zindel, Paul. *The Effect of Gamma Rays on Man-in-the-Moon Marigolds: A Drama in Two Acts.* New York: Bantam Books, 1973.

For information on lectures and workshops or audiotapes contact:

John Lee

West Austin Station

P.O. Box 5892

Austin, TX 78763

or

call 512-445-7992